American Horror Story and Philosophy

Popular Culture and Philosophy® Series Editor: George A. Reisch

Volume 1 *Seinfeld and Philosophy: A Book about Everything and Nothing* (2000)

Volume 2 *The Simpsons and Philosophy: The D'oh! of Homer* (2001)

Volume 3 *The Matrix and Philosophy: Welcome to the Desert of the Real* (2002)

Volume 4 *Buffy the Vampire Slayer and Philosophy: Fear and Trembling in Sunnydale* (2003)

Volume 9 *Harry Potter and Philosophy: If Aristotle Ran Hogwarts* (2004)

Volume 12 *Star Wars and Philosophy: More Powerful than You Can Possibly Imagine* (2005)

Volume 13 *Superheroes and Philosophy: Truth, Justice, and the Socratic Way* (2005)

Volume 17 *Bob Dylan and Philosophy: I's Alright Ma (I'm Only Thinking)* (2006)

Volume 19 *Monty Python and Philosophy: Nudge Nudge, Think Think!* (2006)

Volume 30 *Pink Floyd and Philosophy: Careful with that Axiom, Eugene!* (2007)

Volume 35 *Star Trek and Philosophy: The Wrath of Kant* (2008)

Volume 36 *The Legend of Zelda and Philosophy: I Link Therefore I Am* (2008)

Volume 42 *Supervillains and Philosophy: Sometimes Evil Is Its Own Reward* (2009)

Volume 49 *Zombies, Vampires, and Philosophy: New Life for the Undead* (2010) Edited by Richard Greene and K. Silem Mohammad

Volume 53 *Martial Arts and Philosophy: Beating and Nothingness* (2010) Edited by Graham Priest and Damon Young

Volume 54 *The Onion and Philosophy: Fake News Story True, Alleges Indignant Area Professor* (2010) Edited by Sharon M. Kaye

Volume 55 *Doctor Who and Philosophy: Bigger on the Inside* (2010) Edited by Courtland Lewis and Paula Smithka

Volume 57 *Rush and Philosophy: Heart and Mind United* (2011) Edited by Jim Berti and Durrell Bowman

Volume 58 *Dexter and Philosophy: Mind over Spatter* (2011) Edited by Richard Greene, George A. Reisch, and Rachel Robison-Greene

Volume 60 *SpongeBob SquarePants and Philosophy: Soaking Up Secrets Under the Sea!* (2011) Edited by Joseph J. Foy

Volume 63 *Philip K. Dick and Philosophy: Do Androids Have Kindred Spirits?* (2011) Edited by D.E. Wittkower

Volume 64 *The Rolling Stones and Philosophy: It's Just a Thought Away* (2012) Edited by Luke Dick and George A. Reisch

Volume 67 *Breaking Bad and Philosophy: Badder Living through Chemistry* (2012) Edited by David R. Koepsell and Robert Arp

Volume 68 *The Walking Dead and Philosophy: Zombie Apocalypse Now* (2012) Edited by Wayne Yuen Ralkowski

Volume 71 *The Catcher in the Rye and Philosophy: A Book for Bastards, Morons, and Madmen* (2012) Edited by Keith Dromm and Heather Salter

Volume 73 *The Wire and Philosophy: This America, Man* (2013) Edited by David Bzdak, Joanna Crosby, and Seth Vannatta

Volume 74 *Planet of the Apes and Philosophy: Great Apes Think Alike* (2013) Edited by John Huss

Volume 75 *Psych and Philosophy: Some Dark Juju-Magumbo* (2013) Edited by Robert Arp

Volume 79 *Frankenstein and Philosophy: The Shocking Truth* (2013) Edited by Nicolas Michaud and Jessica Watkins

Volume 80 *Ender's Game and Philosophy: Genocide Is Child's Play* (2013) Edited by D.E. Wittkower and Lucinda Rush

Volume 82 *Jurassic Park and Philosophy: The Truth Is Terrifying* (2014) Edited by Nicolas Michaud

Volume 83 *The Devil and Philosophy: The Nature of His Game* (2014) Edited by Robert Arp

Volume 84 *Leonard Cohen and Philosophy: Various Positions* (2014) Edited by Jason Holt

Volume 86 *Girls and Philosophy: This Book Isn't a Metaphor for Anything.* (2015) Edited by Richard Greene and Rachel Robison-Greene

Volume 87 *Adventure Time and Philosophy: The Handbook for Heroes* (2015) Edited by Nicolas Michaud

Volume 88 *Justified and Philosophy: Shoot First, Think Later* (2015) Edited by Rod Carveth and Robert Arp

Volume 89 *Steve Jobs and Philosophy: For Those Who Think Different* (2015) Edited by Shawn E. Klein

Volume 90 *Dracula and Philosophy: Dying to Know* (2015) Edited by Nicolas Michaud and Janelle Pötzsch

Volume 91 *It's Always Sunny and Philosophy: The Gang Gets Analyzed* (2015) Edited by Roger Hunt and Robert Arp

Volume 92 *Orange Is the New Black and Philosophy: Last Exit from Litchfield* (2015) Edited by Richard Greene and Rachel Robison-Greene

Volume 93 *More Doctor Who and Philosophy: Regeneration Time* (2015) Edited by Courtland Lewis and Paula Smithka

Volume 94 *Divergent and Philosophy: The Factions of Life* (2016) Edited by Courtland Lewis

Volume 95 *Downton Abbey and Philosophy: Thinking in That Manor* (2016) Edited by Adam Barkman and Robert Arp

Volume 96 *Hannibal Lecter and Philosophy: The Heart of the Matter* (2016) Edited by Joseph Westfall

Volume 97 *The Ultimate Walking Dead and Philosophy: Hungry for More* (2016) Edited by Wayne Yuen

Volume 98 *The Princess Bride and Philosophy: Inconceivable!* (2016) Edited by Richard Greene and Rachel Robison-Greene

Volume 99 *Louis C.K. and Philosophy: You Don't Get to Be Bored* (2016) Edited by Mark Ralkowski

Volume 100 *Batman, Superman, and Philosophy: Badass or Boyscout?* (2016) Edited by Nicolas Michaud

Volume 101 *Discworld and Philosophy: Reality Is Not What It Seems* (2016) Edited by Nicolas Michaud

Volume 102 *Orphan Black and Philosophy: Grand Theft DNA* (2016) Edited by Richard Greene and Rachel Robison-Greene

Volume 103 *David Bowie and Philosophy: Rebel Rebel* (2016) Edited by Theodore G. Ammon

Volume 104 *Red Rising and Philosophy: Break the Chains!* (2016) Edited by Courtland Lewis and Kevin McCain

Volume 105 *The Ultimate Game of Thrones and Philosophy: You Think or Die* (2017) Edited by Eric J. Silverman and Robert Arp

Volume 106 *Peanuts and Philosophy: You're a Wise Man, Charlie Brown!* (2017) Edited by Richard Greene and Rachel Robison-Greene

Volume 107 *Deadpool and Philosophy: My Common Sense Is Tingling* (2017) Edited by Nicolas Michaud

Volume 108 *The X-Files and Philosophy: The Truth Is In Here* (2017) Edited by Robert Arp

Volume 109 *Mr. Robot and Philosophy: Beyond Good and Evil Corp.* (2017) Edited by Richard Greene and Rachel Robison-Greene

Volume 110 *Hamilton and Philosophy: Revolutionary Thinking* (2017) Edited by Aaron Rabinowitz and Robert Arp

Volume 111 *The Man in the High Castle and Philosophy: Subversive Reports from Another Reality* (2017) Edited by Bruce Krajewski and Joshua Heter

Volume 112 *The Americans and Philosophy: Reds in the Bed* (2018) Edited by Robert Arp and Kevin Guilfoy

Volume 113 *Jimi Hendrix and Philosophy: Experience Required* (2018) Edited by Theodore G. Ammo

Volume 114 *American Horror Story and Philosophy: Life Is But a Nightmare* (2018) Edited by Richard Greene and Rachel Robison-Greene

In Preparation:

Iron Man vs. Captain America and Philosophy (2018) Edited by Nicolas Michaud and Jessica Watkins

Twin Peaks and Philosophy: That's Damn Fine Philosophy! (2018) Edited by Richard Greene and Rachel Robison-Greene

The Dark Tower and Philosophy (2018) Edited by Nicolas Michaud and Jacob Thomas May

1984 and Philosophy (2018) Edited by Ezio di Nucci and Stefan Storrie

Scott Adams and Philosophy (2018) Edited by Daniel Yim, Galen Foresman, and Robert Arp

Amy Schumer and Philosophy (2018) Edited by Charlene Elsby and Rob Luzecky

For full details of all Popular Culture and Philosophy® books, visit www.opencourtbooks.com.

Popular Culture and Philosophy®

American Horror Story and Philosophy

Life Is But a Nightmare

EDITED BY

RICHARD GREENE AND
RACHEL ROBISON-GREENE

OPEN COURT
Chicago

Volume 114 in the series, Popular Culture and Philosophy®, edited by George A. Reisch

To find out more about Open Court books, visit our website at www.opencourtbooks.com.

Open Court Publishing Company is a division of Carus Publishing Company, dba Cricket Media.

First printing 2018

Printed and bound in the United States of America.

American Horror Story and Philosophy: Life Is But a Nightmare

ISBN: 978-0-8126-9972-2

Library of Congress Control Number: 2017955712

This book is also available as an e-book.

For Alyson Lockwood Petersen

Contents

Thanks

Working on this project has been a pleasure, in no small part because of the many fine folks who have assisted us along the way. In particular, a debt of gratitude is owed to David Ramsay Steele and George Reisch at Open Court, the contributors to this volume, and our respective academic departments at UMass Amherst and Weber State University. Finally, we'd like to thank those family members, students, friends, and colleagues with whom we've had fruitful and rewarding conversations on various aspects of all things *American Horror Story* as it relates to philosophical themes.

The Devil Made Us Write This

What is it that makes *American Horror Story* a truly *American* horror story?

It has something to do with the fact that it is big in a typically American way. For example, the opening sequence of the very first episode contains a creepy house, a shot of some bones, small animal bones hanging from a tree, a set ot twins who, while male, bear a strong resemblance to the twins from *The Shining*, an ominous warning of death from a little girl ("You are going to die in there."), a dilapidated mansion (clearly haunted), a disemboweled cat that is still breathing (clearly haunted), doors that close by themselves, a creepy laboratory with jars containing various human body parts in formaldehyde, some ghosts, and a very bloody murder!

The tone was set from the very beginning. This show is gonna have a lot coming at you all the time. Nearly every moment of every season is full of the kind of passionate intensity reserved for truly apocalyptic and cataclysmic events.

A second feature of *American Horror Story* that serves to make it truly American is the fact that it contains nearly every major trope of American horror stories (perhaps by the time the series has concluded it will include each one). There are vampires, witches, zombies, ghosts, demons, and demonic possession. There is a Frankenstein. There are practitioners of Voodoo. There are crazy hillbillies. They've even got that horny dead guy in the rubber suit. There are haunted houses and hotels. There are legends, cults, freak shows. They've got one of the scariest slasher clowns ever, not to mentioned the murderous gang of clowns in *American Horror Story: Cult*!

The show pays homage to every era of American horror, from the early days of silent horror through creepy B-movie style mental institution and freak show horror of the 1950s and 1960s to modern times, including the horror unleashed by the 2016 election.

Behind all the gore and evil, *American Horror Story* addresses real issues facing Americans today. There is much social commentary on how we treat marginalized groups, and race relations, and civil rights. Strip away the horror and *American Horror Story* is about life in America.

And finally, *American Horror Story* contains a lot of great philosophy! That's where this book comes in. Blood has been spilled to bring about these sixteen chapters. We don't want to claim that our philosophers sold their souls to produce this book, but there's gotta be some explanation.

It cost our writers a whole bunch of blood, toil, tears, and agony. You'd better enjoy it.

I

Goddesses don't speak in whispers. They scream

1
What's So Scary about Demonic Possession?

RACHEL ROBISON-GREENE

The first movie that truly horrified me was *The Exorcist*. It definitely caused some sleepless nights. As an adult, I have a higher scare threshold and I am a big horror fan. I think possession movies are especially fun. So I was thrilled when, early on in *American Horror Story: Asylum*, it was clear that we were going to get a possession story arc, and one that featured Lily Rabe no less.

But there's more to our fear of possession than simply a fear of demons or the Devil. In fact, possession movies are equally creepy for people who don't believe in spirits or supernatural phenomena at all. Let's find out why.

The Devil Comes to Briarcliff

All possession story fans know that uncharacteristic behavior is a telltale sign of demonic possession. Filmmakers tend to like to roll out the unusual behavior slowly, starting with minor behavioral changes. Soon enough though, the possessed person is speaking in languages that they never knew before and eventually begins to speak in a voice that is not their own.

In the second episode of *Asylum*, a terrified family comes to Briarcliff, frantic to obtain help for their teenage son. The young man's behavior had recently started to change. It began with listlessness and depression. They explain that he often wouldn't get out of bed for days. Then, suddenly, the behavior became more terrifying, leading to the moment that his parents heard strange noises coming from the barn. When they investigated the source of the noise, they found their son covered in blood, speaking a language with which the parents were unfamiliar (though, to the demonic possession movie fan, it's clear that it has to be Latin. All demons know Latin). He had ripped open the belly of the parents' prize pig and had eaten its heart.

The boy waits in a room reserved for patients while his parents discuss his case with Sister Jude and Dr. Thredson. Thredson insists that he must see the boy before they attempt anything approaching a diagnosis of his psychological condition. When they enter the room, the boy is sitting on the bed with his hands contorted at an unnatural angle behind his back. When Thredson approaches him to examine him more closely, the boy growls and tries to bite him. His irises change color and he mutters something threatening in Latin. Thredson insists that the boy be medicated immediately. "No doctor," Sister Jude says, knowingly, "that's not what this boy needs." An exorcist is called.

During the exorcism we witness another behavioral change that is common in portrayals of demonic possession in the horror genre. The possessed person suddenly has a vast knowledge base that the body it possesses did not have before. In particular, the demon has all sorts of knowledge about the background of the various parties involved in the exorcism—facts of their lives that the person who appears possessed couldn't possibly know. Features that make it clear that this is not the person it appears to be. It isn't an elaborate scam or trick. The victim couldn't know what this demon knows.

In this case, the possessed boy knows Sister Jude's deep dark secret. He knows that, before she took vows and came to Briarcliff, she was an alcoholic lounge singer who enjoyed the *company* of men. What's worse, he knows that on the way home from a night of carousing, with far too much alcohol in her system, Sister Jude hit a little girl with her car and then sped off into the night. Jude pushed this memory to the back of her mind and managed to move on and reform her life somewhat. The demon, with his god-like omniscience, brings it all back.

The demon also whispers something into the ear of Dr. Thredson that is inaudible at the time. Towards the end of the season we learn what the devil whispered, "You're Bloody Face." The doctor committed the very crimes that the patient he has been sent to evaluate, Kit Walker, is accused of having committed. Now the demon is finished with the body of the boy. He starts frothing at the mouth and is soon dead. The demon has a new vessel in mind.

Sister Mary Eunice is one of the first characters that we meet at the asylum. She is the very stereotype of a nun, diminutive and kind. Dr. Arden, the asylum's physician with a Nazi past and a current research program in eugenics, admires the young nun for her innocence and purity. In fact, it's fair to say that what he feels is more than *admiration*. Her innocence makes her blind to his infatuation with her and to the sinister nature of his character.

Mary Eunice is also willingly submissive to the strict and cruel authority of Sister Jude. When she feels that she has sinned, she begs Sister Jude to lash her. She forms attachments to the patients easily. She weeps when a patient, Willy, dies at the hands of the asylum's Dr. Arthur Arden. Nevertheless, she follows Dr. Arden's every command. She feeds the creatures that he has made out of discarded patients, and, despite the fact that she is not entirely sure what they are, treats them with kindness and compassion.

Sister Mary Eunice's behavior begins to change around the time that the demon leaves the young boy's body. Initially, it is nothing. There seems to be a perpetual smirk on her face that was never there before. Soon she is playing the role of naughty nun and seducing men at Briarcliff whenever it is either convenient or just generally unsettling. Then the body count starts to stack up. It's clear that this isn't the same Mary Eunice we started with. Sister Jude doesn't recognize the devil so easily this time. As Mary Eunice, with great gusto, picks a whip with which to beat Kit and Grace, Jude remarks, "I don't know what's gotten into you lately, Sister, but it's a decided improvement."

I'm Not Who You Think I Am

Most of the time, we take our ability to make basic judgments about personal identity for granted. I drop my son off at school in the morning and pick him up at the end of the day, accepting, without question that I am picking up the same person that I dropped off.

Let's reflect a little on the fundamental importance of these most basic judgments. Imagine how crucial they must have been early on in human development. Human beings are social animals—we need each other to survive. We need to co-operate with one another and we need to co-ordinate to make plans. We need the ability to count on one another. We need to make promises and to rely on one another to keep those promises.

Imagine that you and I live in a community together at an early stage of human development. We come up with a trap to capture a predator that threatens our community. In order to effectively carry out our plan, I need to count on you to be at a particular place at a particular time. To make this happen, I need to be confident that I can judge you to be the same person at the time that we carry out the plan as you were at the time that we made the arrangement. The ability to rely on one another itself relies on consistent judgments of identity through time. We wouldn't have survived as a species without the ability to make consistent identity judgments.

We need the ability to make identity judgments now as much as we ever did. Many of our most crucial human institutions are completely reliant on identity judgments. Consider the practice of holding people morally responsible for their actions. If you were angry with a friend on Tuesday for breaking a promise, you wouldn't be justified in expressing that anger to that friend on your Friday lunch date if, in the time that has passed, something has happened to that person to make them an *entirely different person.* Similarly, if Sister Jude was pleased with Sister Eunice's behavior prior to her possession, she (unknowingly) is not justified in rewarding her when she is no longer Sister Mary Eunice but is, instead, the Devil himself.

On a related note, the human institution of punishment for criminal behavior is also unjustified if we can't make accurate identity judgments across time. I'll provide one real, concrete case that provides a challenge to identity judgments in the real world. In 1969, serial killer Charles Manson convinced members of his "family" (a group of largely young people over whom he exercised control with the use of drugs and his manipulative personality) into murdering a number of people, including, notably, Sharon Tate—movie star and wife of Hollywood director Roman Polanski. Manson family devotees Patricia Krenwinkel, Leslie Van Houten, and Susan Atkins were convicted of the crime.

Krenwinkel, Van Houten, and Atkins demonstrated model prisoner behavior while incarcerated. They have renounced Manson and express great regret for the crimes they committed when they were younger. In 2009, Atkins applied for compassionate release. She had been diagnosed with terminal brain cancer and requested the opportunity to die outside of prison walls. Her request was denied and she died in prison in September 2009. (As I write this, on September 6th 2017, news has broken that Van Houten, just nineteen at the time of the murders in 1969, has been granted parole by the parole board. The Governor may still overturn this decision).

The members of the Manson family weren't possessed by the Devil. They were, however, under the influence of drugs and of the manipulative influence of a sociopath. When both of those influences are absent, are we dealing with different individuals? These are difficult questions. All I want to highlight here is that judgments concerning identity through time are crucial guiding forces (or, at least should be) in our criminal justice system.

There are other human institutions that also rely on identity judgments. How would we understand the concept of property rights if we were unable to make identity judgments? How could we understand power dynamics and relationships of authority? How could we participate in long-term, meaningful relationships? I think the short answer is—we couldn't. That recognition, under the right conditions, is pretty scary.

The Scare Factor

Imagine that you enter a room to find your young daughter, Mary, playing quietly in the corner. You busy yourself tidying up the room. It's just an ordinary scene from an ordinary, fairly standard day in your life. Mary begins to hum a song from your childhood—a song that you are fairly certain Mary couldn't possibly know. You look across the room and notice that Mary is carrying herself differently. The way she is moving is not normal somehow. She looks up and makes eye contact with you. In that moment, you know—*that's not Mary.*

This situation is creepy whether the person occupying Mary's body is a demon or not. The reasons this is frightening are, I think, deep and philosophical, even if we don't realize it as we watch *American Horror Story* from the safety of our own couches. First, we've come to expect that sameness of body is correlated with sameness of person. We each all have a lifetime of experience making (hopefully) accurate identity judgments on the basis of judging a person's body to be the same body from one interaction to the next. What if we couldn't do that? What if the appearance of a person's body told us nothing at all about who is "inside"? That would be deeply unsettling.

Many people believe in the existence of an immortal soul. People who believe in souls tend to believe that we remain the same people through time because we have the same soul through time. Even so, those same people also tend to think that there is some essential connection between body and soul, and it seems that consistency *requires* them to believe in this essential connection. After all, they make judgments that a person is the same person from one moment to the next by observing that the body involved is the same. We can't perceive the existence of sameness of soul, so that couldn't be how the identification is made.

A historical example of a philosopher who held this sort of view was René Descartes. Descartes believed that he was, essentially, a thinking thing—a mind. He also maintained that mind is distinct from body. Famously, Princess Elizabeth of Bohemia challenged Descartes on this view, questioning how a non-physical mind can possibly interact with the physical body. To answer this question, Descartes attempted to develop an account of mind-body "union." Descartes spent much of the remainder of his life trying to tease out the exact nature of this "union." According to his way of thinking, bodies and minds remain distinct. But the relationship between the two is not merely contingent. Body and mind are designed to work together.

Philosophers have raised objections to the soul view of personal identity. For our purposes at this point, it doesn't matter which view, if any, of personal identity is correct. If a person thinks that soul and body bear some sort of essential relationship to one another, that belief is challenged in a frightening way by possession movies and television. The idea that the devil could occupy Sister Mary Eunice's body challenges our own relationships with our own bodies. Maybe we can't count on our own bodies to remain *our* bodies.

Our judgments about identity through time are also crucial to our sense of safety. More than this, these judgments are crucial to our *actual* safety. It can be difficult, at times, to trust other people. Often, when we come to trust others it's because we have witnessed repeated trustworthy behaviors and believe those trustworthy behaviors will continue into the future. It would be difficult to lie down next to your spouse at night if you didn't feel pretty confident that they weren't going to become a homicidal maniac at some point during the night.

Another philosophical theory of what makes a person that person is psychological continuity. A person is the same person from one moment to the next, if and only if they share psychological characteristics in common with their previous self—character traits, memories, and a body of knowledge. When we come to trust other human beings, we have good evidence to believe that those psychological characteristics are the same from one moment to the next.

The knowledge that a person's general psychological profile will remain constant also contributes to our feeling of safety. We could never feel comfortable around anyone if we thought their behavior might change radically at any moment. Consider for a moment the famous case of Phineas Gage. In 1848, Gage was involved in an accident—an iron rod was blown through his face and into his brain. Miraculously, Gage survived the incident, but his behavior changed dramatically. His psychological characteristics became quite different. Before his injury, Gage was mild-mannered and well-respected. Afterward, friends and family described his behavior as animalistic and unpredictable. His mental state changed so dramatically that those closest to him concluded that he was "no longer Gage."

In possession cases, psychological characteristics change all at once. We're no longer in a position to believe that behavior will remain predictable. This explains why we're on the edge of our seats when we, as audience members, are made aware that someone is possessed before any of the show's other characters know. For all we know, the possessed person might suddenly become homicidal. What's more, exorcism stories, when they are good ones like *The Exorcist*, have been known to push the envelope. Homicidal behavior happens all the time in movies of all genres. But exorcism movies sometimes become *truly* unpredictable. Possessed characters do things that make us even *more* uncomfortable. I'll spare you a description, but if you need a description you clearly haven't seen *The Exorcist.* Check it out. Or don't, if you're squeamish. The point is, when we don't know who someone is, we have no good evidence about what they will *do.* Often, the suspense of not knowing what will happen next is more disturbing than what occurs in the scenes with full-blown pea soup barfing, Latin speaking, head spinning exorcisms.

There But for the Grace of God Go I

I've suggested that the fundamental reason that possession storylines are so frightening is that they mess with our ability to make judgments of identity in the case of others. But there is another, more personal reason to be concerned. When identity issues are called into question, we have reason to be less than confident about whether *our own* identity will persist through time.

When I saw *The Exorcist*, I was still a child living with my parents (I saw the movie at a friend's house. I'm sure my parents would not have been thrilled about the movie choice). The access to the attic was right outside my room. If you recall, the Ouija board that led to the whole possession scenario was stored in Regan's attic. After seeing the movie, it was weeks before I was brave enough to leave my room to go to the bathroom or get a drink of water in the middle of the night. I wasn't worried that I'd find Regan walking down the stairs in a backbend. Rather, I was afraid that I would be possessed myself. The fear I felt was a fear that I would no longer be *me*—that my identity would be erased and I would be replaced by a demon. I would cease to exist.

Possession movies poke at our deepest existential anxieties. On some level, we may all be aware that our identities are disturbingly fragile as they are—no demonic threat required. Possession stories are scary because they mess with our ability to make some of our most crucial judgments—judgments about personal identity.

The question of what makes personal identity is a difficult puzzle. We all have the strong intuitive sense that we persist through change. Even though the cells of our body are continually replaced, even though our psychological characteristics change, even though our memories fade and new ones are constantly being formed, we retain our identity through time.

Don't we?

2
A Death Worth Living

ELIZABETH RARD

Most animals are born with an innate fear of death, a fear that is only strengthened by experience and education. When someone we love dies we mourn their loss and are saddened, blaming the evils of death for our pain. When we almost die ourselves we experience terror at the prospect of our demise, and count our lucky stars that we have escaped with out lives.

To humans death is at best an unknown and at worst an end to existence. While we're alive we can experience joy, interact with loved ones, and pursue meaningful goals, but for all we know when we die there is nothing left of us but our rotting corpse.

Much of our rational fear of death is motivated by an attachment to the projects and people that make our lives worth living. It is this fear of leaving behind goals unachieved, and of leaving our loved ones to suffer without us, that inspires our dread. But what if we knew that, were we to die in a certain location, our consciousness would continue to exist? What if we had a chance to exist forever in a way that would allow us to continue to pursue out goals and interact with the people closest to us? Would it not be better to live forever than to cease to exist?

In the magical and terrifying universe of *American Horror Story*, especially the universe that the Murder House and the Hotel Cortez exist in, people have the opportunity to exist forever, albeit as ghosts who have technically died. People who die in certain places, on the grounds of a haunted house or haunted hotel for instance, will come back as ghosts, cursed (or blessed) with the opportunity to haunt the building they died in for a potentially never-ending tenure.

The extent to which they retain their memories and identity from before their death varies, as does their ability to move on from old obsessions. Nora, who wanders the basement of the Murder House unable to remember that she has died, is forever fixated on acquiring a baby even though she does not enjoy the realities of motherhood. Hayden, who remembers that she is dead, and can even recall the details of her death, is nonetheless fixated on sleeping with and then killing as many men as she can, as she tries continually to work out frustrations left over from her time among the living.

But for others death is an opportunity to achieve new goals and to grow as humans beyond the people they were when they died. Sally, who spent years feeling empty for her lack of true human connection, finds new meaning when she is given a cell phone and a Twitter account. She finds new purpose in her relationship with her Internet fans, purpose that allows her to grow as a person. As a ghost Mr. March is able to complete a project that was important to him in life but was left unfinished at the time of his death. Of course his project involved the killing of many, many innocent (or maybe not so innocent) people, but it is still a meaningful accomplishment for him.

The problem is that forever is a pretty long time, and if the ghosts who reside in the Murder House and the Hotel Cortez are to continue to have afterlives worth living, they're going to need to find a way to fend off the impending boredom of eternity.

Dead but Not Gone

There are two disturbing possibilities that are largely responsible for our fear of death. The first possibility is that there is nothing after we die, that we simply cease to exist.

The second possibility is that we will exist in some form after we die, and that our existence will be horrible (Fione Goode waking up dead at the end of Season Three, surrounded by knotted pine).

While there are other possible outcomes after we die, these are the two that make death such a potential harm. Let's focus first on the possibility that there will be nothing after we die, as many reasons to fear death are motivated specifically by this possibility. We find meaning in our lives by cultivating relationships with other people, and by engaging in worthwhile projects. Dying, and especially dying young, robs us of the opportunity to finish our projects. It cuts short the relationships that we have, and it leaves our loved ones behind without the comfort of our presence. It seems that it's better to die when we are old and have achieved many of our goals, perhaps even when there are fewer people left around to miss us. People often talk of wanting to complete some life goal or project before they die. If there's nothing after we die then our desire to be around for our loved ones and to achieve our goals really does give us a good reason to fear and avoid death.

But what if we were to find ourselves on the property of the Murder House, or the (less crowded and more spacious) Hotel Cortez? Many of the traditional reasons to avoid death would no longer concern us. For example when Doctor Ben Harmon considers killing himself in the Murder House, he has good reasons to want to die on the premises, and, because he knows he will come back as a ghost, he has less reason to avoid death than we do. A good portion of his family has already perished in the Murder House. His wife and daughter, even his near stillborn infant child, are all now continuing to exist as ghosts in the house. If he dies on the property he can continue to have a relationship with his family.

In addition Doctor Harmon can still work towards the goals that made his life meaningful prior to his death. While Ben Harmon may have struggled with his commitment to his marriage at times, he has always been committed to his patients. As a ghost in the Murder House Ben will have many opportunities to help other people (many of them ghosts) work through their issues. Chad and Patrick could definitely use some marriage counseling. Tate has repressed memories and more than a little guilt that he could use some help processing. And clearly Hayden has some anger and abandonment issues to work through (although Ben might have difficulty maintaining professional detachment with Tate and Hayden). In addition the quick turn-around of residents coming through the house guarantees Ben a near constant stream of potential new patients.

What about our second concern, that continued existence after death might involve some unthinkable horror? Again, from Ben's perspective killing himself in the house gives him the best chance of avoiding an unknown afterlife. He has observed many people die on the premises and continue to exist as ghosts, and although some of them are miserable, he believes that his dead wife Vivien, and their daughter Violet, are actually relatively happy. It is reasonable for Ben to choose a known situation, one in which he can pursue meaningful goals and be with his family, over the uncertainty of eventually dying outside of the Murder House. Of course Ben chooses life, in large part because he feels an obligation to care for his wife's other child. But when Ben is killed as he attempts to leave the house, and as we see the peace Ben finds when he is finally able to have the relationship with his family as a ghost that has so long evaded him as a living person, we cannot help but feel that Ben is getting a happy ending, especially given that the baby he was leaving with turned out to be the demonic fruits of an unholy union between the living and the dead.

Bored to Death

Death is largely taken to be a harm because it prevents us from completing our projects, and we will be missed by our loved ones. If, however, we die on a haunted property and return as a ghost, then death has not robbed us of our relationships and projects—unless, of course, our projects involve mountain climbing or windsurfing. As such, dying to become a ghost is not harmful in the same way that dying with no hope of an afterlife is. But this does not necessarily mean that becoming a ghost is a good thing. We never find out what will happen to a ghost if the building they are haunting is destroyed. It is only hinted that they might move on or cease to exist. But let's assume that our ghosts could know that the buildings they haunt will always stand, and that their consciousness will always reside within the buildings. Could eternity as a ghost actually be a good thing? After all, eternity is pretty long.

If you die in a haunted building in the *American Horror Story* Universe you basically become immortal, and immortality has the rather disturbing potential to be incredibly boring. Bernard Williams once argued that death at an old age, with no possibility of an afterlife, is a good thing. This was because he thought that if we live too long eventually we will lose all of the goals and desires that make life worth living. Williams said that, since we need meaningful projects to make life meaningful, and meaningful projects are finite in scope, immortality would be a harm because eventually our lives would become meaningless.

Imagine that Ben treats all of the people living in the Murder House and eventually they all become happy, well-adjusted ghosts. And in addition at some point people wise up and stop moving into the Murder House. At this point Ben will no longer have the project, to make his life meaningful, of helping people. He will need to replace this goal with another. Perhaps he can learn to paint. But at some point (perhaps after hundreds or even thousands of years) Ben will become a master painter. What shall he do then? Learn another language? Then learn all the languages? Every project will be finished at some point, and eventually Ben will simply run out of projects. To complicate the issue, Williams argued that it is the specific projects that we invest our time in that make us who we are. If we change our goals substantially we will no longer be the same person, and this is itself a kind of death.

The Time of Your Life

One way to (at least) prolong the meaningfulness of our projects is to pursue multiple open-ended projects. Perhaps treating patients isn't enough to give Ben's life meaning, but Ben has other goals as well. He has a goal of protecting people from the Murder House. If we assume that people continue to move into the house (it is a reasonably priced home with gorgeous Tiffany fixtures, after all) then this is a meaningful project that Ben could continue to pursue indefinitely. In addition, maintaining a good relationship with loved ones can be a meaningful goal, one that requires regular action to achieve. It seems likely that there will never be a point where Ben's relationship with Violet, for example, will be finished. Rather he will need to continue to work at maintaining that connection.

Near the end of Season Five, Liz also considers death in a haunted location, this time on the grounds of the Hotel Cortez. In a beautiful scene Liz asks her friends, who she considers her family, to help her end her life so that she can become a ghost and stay with them forever. At this point Liz has been diagnosed with terminal cancer and so she really is choosing between death outside the hotel, with all the corresponding uncertainty, and immortality as a ghost. After her death Liz is reunited with the love of her life, Tristan. He says that the reason he never appeared to her when she was still alive is that Liz still had more living to do. When Liz becomes a ghost she has achieved everything she needed to in order to be at peace as a ghost. She became strong and confident in her identity, she has established a relationship with her son, one that they can continue after her death, and she has created a family for herself in the hotel. She becomes a ghost with no lingering projects that cannot be completed after her death.

In addition to being surrounded by friends and loved ones there are two other key factors that give us hope that she will continue to live a meaningful death. Before she died Liz ensured that the Hotel Cortez would be safe. With the help of Iris and Mr. March, she convinces the ghosts to stop killing the guests, so that the hotel can once again have a regular stream of clients to sustain it. In addition, she inspires Will Drake to begin to design again, so that money from his business can help to maintain the hotel. She has saved the hotel and given its residents new purpose and after her death she will continue to serve as a protector of the hotel and its guests. This is a pursuit that is largely open-ended. It will require that Liz continue to manage the behavior of other ghosts in the hotel by helping them to find renewed meaning in their own existence.

Liz also has a connection to the outside world through her son, and his newborn child, that can conceivably give meaning to her life indefinitely. She can continue to see her son and his child, interact with them as a ghost, as they live their lives. If Liz's grandchild has children Liz can develop a relationship with them as well, and so on down through the generations. Each life that Liz interacts with will be different and unique, each relationship she builds will be novel, and will provide added meaning to her existence. In this way Liz can have an immortal existence as meaningful as any mortal life.

We see the relationship of meaning and goals, and the dangers of completing those goals, most clearly with Mr. March. March was an ambitious man while he was alive and when he ended his life (albeit without any inkling that he would return as a ghost) he continued the projects that gave his life meaning. The two projects that initially consume him in his afterlife are the pursuit of the Countess, who was his wife but who never loved him, and the completion of his masterpiece, which involved killing quite a few people in various gruesome ways, more or less related to the Ten Commandments.

Mr. March thinks that if he gives the Countess everything she wants, eliminates all his rivals, and prevents her from leaving the hotel, he can have the love that he has desired for so long. When the Countess is finally dead and can no longer flee the hotel it becomes clear to Mr. March that she will never love him. The hope that one day he could manipulate her into loving him was one part of his meaningful existence as a ghost. When he finally has her where he wants her, trapped in the hotel, he realizes that this goal is unachievable, and that knowledge makes any further pursuit meaningless. It would perhaps be better to pursue a meaningless goal blindly than to be forced to give up in the face of reality.

Another of his projects ends about the same time, although he does not seem quite as disheartened by its resolution. For years after his death Mr. March has searched for a successor, someone worthy to finish his Ten Commandments killings. While others (including John Wayne Gacy and Richard Ramirez) have failed to be the protégé he sought, John Lowe is finally able to follow in his footsteps, completing his masterpiece. Again a project that had brought meaning to Mr. March's life is completed, only this time Mr. March seems to find comfort in the closure. One reason that Mr. March is able to continue to lead a meaningful life is that he becomes involved with, and invested in, new projects. Specifically he becomes invested in the future of the hotel. He helps Liz to motivate the ghosts to play by the rules so that the hotel, which is another part of his legacy, can eventually become a protected landmark, thus insuring that it will continue to stand.

The afterlife is a very long time, and without meaningful and engaging projects and relationships to get us through we are doomed to an eternity of unbearable boredom. Will the sorts of projects that the ghosts of the *American Horror Story* universe have adopted be enough to keep them busy forever? Only time will tell.

Cleaning Up

While open-ended meaningful projects may be able to keep us sustained for longer periods of time than finite projects there is another option that would guarantee a meaningful existence for any amount of time. Richard Taylor argues that a life full of repetitive mundane tasks can be just as meaningful as a life filled with grandiose projects, provided that the person performing the tasks took the tasks to be meaningful and enjoyable. Sisyphus, who was cursed to roll the same bolder up a hill over and over for all eternity, would have a meaningful life as long as he decided that he wanted to keep rolling that bolder up the hill, and believed his task to be meaningful. As long as we believe our projects are meaningful they will be meaningful to us, which is what is required to have a worthwhile existence.

The Laundress who resides in the hotel, and has devoted her life to Mr. March, seems to find endless joy in scrubbing rugs, bleaching linens, and washing towels. She is thrilled every time a mess is made, for the purpose of her existence seems to be nothing more than to clean up the various horrific messes created by the hotel's many occupants. We get the sense that she really could have been happy steaming drapes for all eternity. Alas her joy is greatly diminished when she confesses her love to Mr. March, only to be met with distain. And, given that the ghosts have agreed to be on their best behavior, truly gruesome stains are becoming harder to come by. However we can imagine that, had she never confessed her love, and had the murders continued on at a good pace, the Laundress might have continued to find meaning in her daily tasks until the end of time.

As she says "there are more stains in heaven and earth than are dreamt of in your philosophy."

3
My Sister, My Self?

RICHARD GREENE

One afternoon back in 1952 I wandered in to a matinee performance at Fräulein Elsa's Cabinet of Curiosities. This, of course, is the fancy name Elsa Mars gave to what used to be called a "freak show."

I saw many acts. Some were most unusual (some were not so unusual). There was a set of conjoined twins (one body, two necks, two heads!), a bearded lady, a strongman, a young fellow with hands that were shaped like lobster claws, the world's shortest woman (twenty-five inches tall!), a woman they said was a "pinhead" (I don't think this a very nice term), a lady that had three breasts, and a whole slew of others. There was also a really creepy clown in a filthy and tattered outfit milling about, but I don't think that he was actually part of the show. I can't say that I enjoyed the show much: the facilities were run down, the performers seemed sad and defeated, and their acts weren't particularly entertaining—mostly they were just there to be gawked at.

After the show, however, I wandered behind the big tent to the area where the performers were eating their supper, and I saw something that really captured my attention! In fact, it has occupied my thoughts ever since. It was a wonderful conversation between Dot and Bette (the conjoined twins) and some of the other entertainers. I present the conversation here for your consideration as faithfully I can recall it.

Richard Greene

That's One Freaky Ship

Jimmy Darling (the lobster boy): What's that you're reading, Bette?

Dot: I'm sure she's reading something she can later use to annoy me.

Bette: It's philosophy! Since getting out of mother's house, I've learned things about the world that I never knew existed. My world (our world) used to be so small, but now the possibilities seem endless. This got me thinking: I should learn about other things. I've been reading about faraway places, other civilizations, movie stars, and lately philosophy. This article is about the Ship of Theseus.

Ma Petite (the world's shortest woman): Ship of what?

Bette: Ship of Theseus! It's from Greek mythology.

Jimmy Darling: Tell us about it.

Dot: Please don't!

Bette: Okay. From what I've read, there are many different versions of the story of the Ship of Theseus, but the idea is something like this. Suppose that in Ancient Greece the citizens of Athens built this war ship, and the named it the Ship of Theseus. It was made mostly of wood, and it was a thing of real beauty. The Athenians were committed to keeping it intact, so whenever some of the wood decayed, they replaced it with a piece that was identical to the original piece. Let me get your opinions on this. After they replaced the first piece, do you think it was still the same ship?

Jimmy Darling: Sure

Ma Petite: Of course.

Dell Toledo (the strong man): I suppose.

Bette: Great. We all agree. That's what pretty much everyone thinks. And if they replace a few more pieces. It would still be the same ship. Right? [*Everyone seems to agree.*] But if they replace every piece slowly over time, then it's not so clear that it is the same ship. This is where folks start to disagree. If every piece has been replaced, some think it can't be the same ship, and others think that it's still the same ship. It's a real paradox. If you don't think it's the same ship anymore, just because every part has been replaced, then you have to explain why not. People change over time—every cell in your bodies has died and has been replaced by new cells many times in your lives.

You also have to identify the exact point at which it stopped being the same ship. Is it at fifty percent, seventy-five percent, some other point? It all seems kind of arbitrary. On the other hand, if you think it's the same ship even after all the parts have been replaced, what do you say about this twist? Suppose that someone kept all the original parts, and once they had the entire set, they put them back together in the original form. Now you have two ships: The one that has all the new parts, and the one with the original parts. They can't both be the ship of Theseus, can they?

But it seems like the one with the original parts has the stronger claim. It's just as if Jimmy took his motorcycle apart and then put it back together again. It's still the same motorcycle, isn't it? And did the one with the replacement parts stop being the ship that it had been for years, just because someone put the other one back together? That seems really wrong!

Ma Petite: Soooo . . . what's the right answer?

Bette: That's the thing. The philosophers can't seem to agree on it. Like I said, it's a real paradox.

It's a Better Bike Now, But It's Not a Different Bike

Dot: [*to Bette*] Okay, I've heard enough. I don't care about philosophy. I don't see why you care about philosophy. And I don't see how philosophy has anything to do with me.

Jimmy Darling: I think it's pretty interesting. It's fun to think about.

BETTE: It's more than just interesting, Jimmy. Dot is wrong; it's about us, all of us.

DELL TOLEDO: How, so, Bette? I don't see it.

BETTE: Well, Dell, we are all kinda like the Ship of Theseus. As I said, over time all of our parts have changed—they've been replaced—but we are still the same persons that we've always been.

MA PETITE: But I'm not the same person I used to be. When I was little, um littler, I was twelve inches tall, now I'm twenty-five inches tall. When I was younger I wanted to be a great detective, but now I don't want that, I like being an entertainer. When I was a child, I didn't like eating my vegetables, but now I love them. How am I the same?

BETTE: To say that you are the same isn't to deny that you've changed. I know that sounds weird, but think about it this way. Before Jimmy gave his bike that great new paint job, it was blue. Now it's red. So, it changed, but it's still the same motorcycle. The bike itself didn't change. It was the properties of the bike that changed. Similarly, Ma Petite, you've been the same person your whole life, but features of you are different. Your tastes, your dreams, your physical attributes, etc. can change, and you can still stay the same.

MA PETITE: I see.

BETTE: What a lot of philosophers think is that we are the same persons over time because of something like our memories. We have a psychological history that connects us to our past selves. It's because they are *my* memories, that make me the same person now that I was when I was younger. The problem with this approach, though, is that not everyone has this continuous psychological history. Consider the case of someone who has been in a coma for a long time. Presumably they are the same person they were before the coma, even though they stopped having memories, or any thoughts at all, a long time ago.

Or consider someone who has lost all their memories, or someone who has nothing but false memories, or someone who has gone into a coma, and then come out of it. These poor folks don't meet the continuous psychological history requirement, but it seems crazy to say that they aren't the same person over time. Also, what about things that don't have memories? Jimmy's motorcycle is still the same motorcycle. That worm on the ground is still the same worm. So, for most things, they can and do change a lot, but we still think they're the same thing. Like I said, it's a real paradox. Frankly, it's very troubling.

Know Thyself (or at Least Know What Thou Art)

Desiree Dupree (the three-breasted lady): I see why you think that it's about all of us. I suppose that most philosophy is in one way or another. But why is it troubling? Isn't this all just a matter of how we choose to categorize things? The way we talk about things? I once was the hired entertainment at a weekend long philosophy conference. I don't know why they wanted a three-breasted lady to sing and dance for them, but I guess it's because there weren't any women invited. I don't know. At any rate, they were all talking about this fellow named "Quine" or something. This Mr. Quine apparently thought that things such as persons aren't real. The individual parts are real—I guess that means our atoms are real—but the collections of parts aren't real. So I'm not the same person as I used to be, because I wasn't that person either. It's just parts that ever existed. Some of them still exist, some don't. But it's very convenient for us to speak of things the way we do.

Bette: You said a couple of different things there, Desiree. The stuff about only parts of things really existing, is a view that some philosophers hold. It may be right. I know that folks worry about that view because it creates a lot of problems for making sense of things like consciousness, among other things. But the other thing you said, is the one I want to address. You asked why it troubles me. I guess my answer is that if you, or Ma Petite, or Jimmy, or even Elsa, for that matter, can't sort out these issues, it's no big deal, but if Dot and I can't solve these issues, how are we going to know exactly what we are? How are we going to answer questions about ourselves? It's very disconcerting.

Dot: What are you talking about Bette?

Bette: Dot, I don't have any idea what the hell we are!

Dot: It's easy—we are conjoined twins. We are sisters. We are stuck with each other.

Bette: It's not that simple. I have a whole bunch of questions that I'd like to have answered, but mainly, I'd like to know whether we are one person or two.

Dot: Why wouldn't you think that we are two persons?

Bette: Let's start with our physical stuff. According to the doctor at the hospital we went to when you stabbed me, we don't have two completely different sets of parts. It might be easier to sort out if we were two whole entities that were just fused together—joined at the hip, as they say. But we have one bladder, three kidneys, four lungs, two hearts, one reproductive system, one circulatory system, and two brains. Hell, when I smoke a cigarette, the smoke comes out of your mouth.

Dot: That doesn't seem problematic to me. What makes us different is the fact that we have different brains and different minds. We have different thoughts and different memories, even if we remember a lot of the same things, the way in which we remember them is different. The way we feel about our memories is different. That stuff you were saying before about our psychological histories seems relevant here.

Bette: Maybe you're right, but you can't ignore all the things we share. If we are just our minds, then our other parts are not really part of us. Remember when we were five and mother gave us that doll for our birthday? I think it *might* be right to say that there was a toy that we both owned, but that doll didn't haven't anything to do with who we are.

I'm not ready to say it's the same thing with our shared body parts. We aren't the co-owners of some legs, and a circulatory system, and so forth. I don't think we are just our brains. More importantly, we can't just be our minds. What if you slipped into a coma, and no longer had consciousness? Would you cease to exist? What if you had been born without consciousness at all, like an encephalic baby. Wouldn't everyone want to say that I just had two brains, one that worked, and one that didn't? Just as if one of my lungs didn't work. I don't know why the right thing to say isn't just that we are a single thing, one that happens to have two brains and two minds. I mean, if I bought a radio and it had two separate receiver/transmitter set-ups, say one for private conversations and one for short wave conversations, you wouldn't say that I had two radios, would you?

Dell Toledo: I think Bette might be right about this. I read about some experiments that these brain doctors were doing. They figured out the brain has two sides: the left side and the right side. I think they called them "hemispheres." These two parts of the brain are connected by these string-like things called the "corpus callosum." These doctors were trying to help epileptics—keep them out of Fräulein Elsa's Cabinet of Curiosities, so to speak, so they severed their patients' corpus callosums, and, you won't believe it, but the patients ended up with two personalities. It seems that if you split someone's brain they can end up with two minds—two consciousnesses. At least that's how some of the brainiacs interpret it. I think this shows that it's at least possible for one body to have two minds.

Bette: Right! Also, are you sure that we have two minds, Dot? Don't you think it's a little weird that we can communicate without speaking?

Jimmy Darling: What?!?

Ma Petite: How do you do that?

Desiree Dupree: Are you telling me that you two can talk to each other behind our backs right in front of our faces?

Dot: Great job, letting the cat out of the bag, Bette. If you were wondering why I stabbed you . . .

BETTE: Yes, Dot and I are telepathic. We can communicate by thinking things to one another. I'm not sure how it works, but it provides us with some reason for thinking that we are of a single mind.

DOT: But, if we are of a single mind, why can't you read all my thoughts. I know what you think about most things because your behavior tells me, but I never know exactly what you're thinking unless you send your thoughts to me. That seems to suggest that we are two minds, but minds that have a way of interacting.

BETTE: Maybe. Maybe not. Psychologists tell us that we have a conscious part to our mind and an unconscious part. No one knows what the unconscious part knows, if it knows anything at all, but we know that conscious parts of the mind are not aware of what the unconscious parts are doing. On top of that, some philosophers and psychologists think that our minds have lots of parts, they use words like "ego," "superego," "id," rational or logical part," "appetitive part," "spirited part," "reason," and "passions." It's really unclear what to say about any of this. But you definitely can't conclude from the fact that we seem to have two minds that we do have two minds, and even if we do have two minds, it isn't obvious that we are two separate things. Like I keep saying, it's a real paradox!

DOT: Fine. But what about this? I've heard stories about conjoined twins being separated. Suppose that happened to us. It's simple logic to point out that we would be two distinct people. For example, I might travel to San Francisco, and you might travel to New York City. Anyone that claimed that we were still the same person would have to hold that a single thing could be in two places at once. That's impossible. And if you say that we become two people upon being separated, which one of us is the original and which one is the new person? Also, it would be pretty weird to be a brand-new person that is fully developed, with a whole set of memories, desires, and preferences, etc. It is much easier and makes more sense to me, to think that we were two persons the whole time.

BETTE: Maybe there is no right answer. I just don't know what to say. I do know that I don't want to embrace a view just because it is easier to hold that view. Sometimes the things that make the most sense, at least on an intuitive level, turn out to be the most wrong. Is there anything to rule out the possibility that we are currently one person, but upon separation become two, each with all the memories and things you just mentioned? I don't know if I think that is right, but it certainly isn't as worrisome as the alternatives you just presented.

DOT: Okay, I've got one final argument. What about the fact that this whole time we've been using language that suggests that we are two separate persons. We say things like "*We* say things," and "*You* believe this, but *I* believe that," "*Bette* is nicer than *Dot*," and so on. Doesn't the language we use reveal to us facts about the way the world really is?

BETTE: Yes, sometimes it does, but not when it comes to abstract philosophical stuff. Remember that Mr. Quine pointed out that we use language in a certain way to refer to things because it is convenient to do so. But that leaves open the question of whether those things aren't real, or that reality is one way or another. Again, I just don't know. [*Elsa enters the dining area*]

ELSA: Okay, troupe, we have our evening show coming up in thirty minutes. Get to your trailers to prepare right away. Tonight I'm singing "Life on Mars" again, and you don't want to miss it!"

So Many Questions?

Well, dear reader, that's the conversation I witnessed. It started me on a journey of self-discovery that exposed me to history of philosophy, psychology, and even neuroscience. It led me to consider deeper questions about the nature of mind, the nature of consciousness, personal identity, persistence of objects over time, the nature of persons, human motivation, and many other topics. My hope is that this conversation will inspire you in similar ways.

4
How to Live through a Horror Story and Still Find Your Self

JACOB BROWNE AND CHRISTOPHE POROT

It's a strange world we live in. There are things out there that we don't understand, things that belong only somewhere like *American Horror Story*.

None of us *really* wants to see stuff like that spill off the screen into our world. Even if we enjoy watching them, it'd be pretty terrible if anyone were to find themselves in an episode. How might someone get through a thing like that? Well, most of us who watch horror movies would suggest a few of the usual ground rules: don't panic, don't go off on your own, and don't go in "there." But there's more help to be found, from an unexpected source. Not the Ghostbusters, but Canadian philosopher, Charles Taylor.

Taylor's the best guide through any *American Horror Story* (or *Horror Story of Any Other Given Nationality*) because he can explain all about what kind of Selves there are. To understand the world you're in, it's handy to understand what your Self is like. As they say, "You better check yourself before you wreck yourself."

Self, World, and Story

For Charles Taylor, our sense of Self and the world we live in are stitched together more tightly than the twisted creations of any mischievous witch or mad surgeon (apologies to *Coven*'s Kyle and *Murder House*'s Thaddeus).

Taylor sees humans as creatures who constantly interpret their environment, seeing meaning in things sometimes even before they've recognized them. For Taylor and philosophers like him, the meaning we find in the world, the things we imagine to be surrounding us, all depend on our own state of mind, the kind of world we *feel* like we're living in. So, if someone's fearful, they might look for a knife-wielding maniac in every shadow, whether they're there or not. Or, if they're in a hopeful mood, they might see possibilities everywhere, and perhaps miss a few danger signs. Think of the Harmons and the Millers, when they move into the *Roanoke* and *Murder Houses*, sticking around despite the multiple murder attempts. In either case, hopeful or fearful, they have a "mood" or an "attunement" that makes reality "disclose" different possibilities and alternative meanings to them.

Reality may "disclose" different things to different people, says Taylor. It all depends on this "attunement" business, this stuff about your pre-existing emotional and psychic state, and what that means about how you see and interpret the world. And that depends on just who you are, what's important to you, what you know about. In other words, it depends on your Self. That's not necessarily because you see "neutral" reality, and then impose your own thing onto it. Reality isn't something we always find raw, and then mentally carve up and flavor with our own imposed meanings. Sometimes, the meal arrives fully cooked, even partially digested, on your figurative dinner plate. You've already begun tucking in, before you even realized it was feeding time. The point where the "meaning" of reality can be found—where the meal is cooked and the "flavoring" gets in—depends on your Self.

This means there's no division of "inside" our heads and "out there" in the world. For Taylor, consciousness and reality just can't be separated. Those who insist that it can are falling for an illusion. Remember the trick that goes so wrong for the magician, Chester (actually, more disastrously wrong for Maggie) in "*Freak Show:* Show Stoppers"? Where the lady in the box gets sawn in half? Trying to separate our being and the world is a bit like that. It's either a bit of sleight-of-hand, with no real separation, just the illusion of one; or things get violent, there are metaphysical entrails all over the stage, and the being you were trying to divide up is *definitely* not in the world anymore.

Different attunements might make two people see the same thing in different ways. Think of the first hours of *Return to Roanoke* ("*Roanoke:* Chapter Six"), before things start going off-kilter. The actors (Audrey, Monet, Rory and Dominic) find themselves in an attractive colonial-style farmhouse, where they'll star in a reality television program. They see an adoring audience behind every surface, or the mischievous hand of the show's producer, Sidney. But the original Roanokers (Matt, Shelby and Lee) must be seeing torrents of blood, the flicker of flaming torches and the possibility of death wherever they look. Same house, different experience of reality. A more extreme example? Moira of the *Murder House* is of the sultry, lingerie-clad variety of housemaid to the virile and intermittently adulterous Ben Harmon. To anyone but a heterosexual male, she's a bit older, and somewhat less seductive.

The lusty gaze of Ben Harmon tells us something else about the interconnections of Self, attunement, and reality. If they functioned like an animal instinct—something preprogrammed and inescapable—Ben's reality would be fixed. His attunement would *always* highlight what his libido tells him is 'important.' He'd be like a frightened deer. Reality for the deer always seems just about to disclose a snapped twig, the tangy odor of a predator, the soft click of a loading rifle. Ben is "attuned" to desire, not fear, so reality-with-Moira-in-it is unbearably full of whispered possibilities of rustling silks, a delicate scent in the air, and the warmth of skin brushing against skin. This is the stuff that jumps out of reality at him, the things he sees whether he's consciously looking for them or not.

But Ben's a human being, with self-awareness and a proper capacity for language. For Taylor, this makes him a "Self-Interpreting Animal." Ben can make further evaluations about what's 'important' in the world, and re-interpret his experience. So, he can *alter* his attunement. Sure, on some level, he wants to get to know Moira more intimately. But equally, he doesn't want to want that. He wants to want only his wife, Vivien. He thinks he shouldn't notice every time Moira's undergarments are exposed. Gradually, his attunement changes. Eventually, he's not a red-blooded male anymore. He's a faithful husband. Remember how entwined being and the world are? When his Self changes, so does his world. Finally, with a valiant effort, he stops seeing sexy-Moira, and sees her less desirable alter-ego.

You, too, are a Self-Interpreting Animal. This is important—it shows that you're definitely in *some* kind of story. This is because a Self always has to be structured across time to have meaning, somehow uniting the past, the present and the future into one interpretation. Narratives provide that structure by tying together all these things. They make events meaningful, and not just "one thing after another." Because of this, a Self-Interpreting Animal is always a Self-Narrating Animal. If this is news to you, welcome to your own story!

Porous Self, Enchanted Cosmos

Since Self and world are so intertwined, Taylor talks about them as part of a historical narrative, a story about how a medieval "enchanted cosmos" turned into the modern "disenchanted universe." Linked to those was a change, for most people, from a sense of the Self as "porous" to a sense of the Self as "buffered." Porous and buffered selves see themselves as living in different kinds of worlds, with different rules and parameters—hence the transition described by Taylor's historical narrative. Let's start with the first stage, the "enchanted cosmos."

To begin with, when things were "enchanted," the whole planet, the sky and heavens looked different. The earthly realm where humans live was at the center of a series of spheres. Humans lived on the lowest and most imperfect one, but everything above that realm got more perfect, until you reached the absolute perfection of God at the highest point. There was supposed to be an incredibly deep interaction between all these revolving spheres and all things within them. Everything had its place, fitting seamlessly into the whole. The planets literally sang as they made their way through the firmament. Horror movie buffs who would like a graphic illustration of this universe and an exploration of some of its implications should check out Benjamin Christensen's 1922 movie, long banned in the United States, *Häxan: Witchcraft Throughout the Ages*, a cult silent semi-documentary about spells, Satanic worship, and society.

The writer C.S. Lewis described this universe as "tingling with anthropomorphic life, dancing, ceremonial, a festival not a machine." Looking up was like looking into a great cathedral. Man was just one part of that grand hierarchical system. Everything was "enchanted" because it did its own thing, had its own meaning, independent of humankind. It was what Taylor calls an "ordered cosmos."

Because every section was constantly interacting with the others, there were many different kinds of things that could act upon humans. You get a sense of this with modern astrology and star signs, which are an adaptation of medieval beliefs. But it wasn't just celestial bodies that influenced our characters, behaviors and fortunes. Angels had their own sphere, independent from ours, just below God's. Like Shachath, the merciful Angel of Death who appears in the *Asylum*, they sometimes affected human affairs, but weren't part of them. More importantly for you and your Horror Story, spirits and demons also had their place. They could enter into us from the outside, stealing our willpower, making us do terrible things. The demon in *Asylum*'s Sister Mary Eunice is heir to a long tradition that was at its strongest in the time of the "ordered cosmos."

There were even stranger things capable of influencing human affairs, if you were attuned to them. Like inanimate objects, bits of dead people, or even places. Touching the finger-bone of a saint or travelling to a place where a miracle happened might give you a nice boost of health, and a better moral character, too. The power of influence went that deep.

And it wasn't just holy things that could change you. Objects could be cursed, like the rubber suit in the Murder House, which brings havoc whenever it appears. More powerful still was the force that a place could exert. What does the psychic Billie Dean Howard tell Violet in *Murder House*:

> The evil . . . is real and powerful. Created by events. Events that unleash psychic energy into the environment, where it's absorbed. . . . You'll see it all the time in places like prisons or asylums. Negative energy feeds on trauma and pain. It draws those things to it. The force here in this house is larger than the many individual traumas. And it has a need. It wants to break through. It wants to move in our world.

In every season except for *Freak Show*, we see the history of a place bursting into the present, as if blood spilt long ago were perpetually crying out for fresh blood. Once a place has been tainted, its evil emanates into everything that comes near. If it doesn't directly make a human in that place more evil, it may still bring serious harm to them. The Roanoke and Murder Houses, the Briarcliff Asylum, and the Hotel Cortez all have sordid secrets in their pasts, and all have uncanny effects on anyone unfortunate enough to visit.

The Self-understanding of humans in the "enchanted" world reflected all of these cosmological details, since Self and world are so closely tied together. The big difference is about how the lines are drawn around the Self. Your entire life—your character, your fortunes and misfortunes, your decisions and actions—was attuned to mysterious influences from the whole order of nature, from the planetary to the personal. As Taylor puts it, "Influence does away with sharp boundaries." So the Self in the enchanted world was a very fuzzy thing, like a kind of sponge, absorbing all these forces. Using Taylor's preferred word, it was "porous."

Buffered Self, Disenchanted Universe

The world became disenchanted through a whole swarm of different processes. You might be thinking that science had something to do with it, and you wouldn't be completely wrong. But it's not just modern rational science beating old-fashioned superstition and ignorance. It's about a change in the way we thought about ourselves and our relation to the world. It's another re-interpretation, like with Ben and Moira above, a gradual change in attunement. In short, it's a change in the Self and its reality.

Sure, scientific discoveries happened as a result of that change, but in a way, they were more effect than cause. Scientists had to make a kind of "inward" turn to make these breakthroughs. They had to imagine their minds as "disengaged" from the world, separate from what they were observing. A kind of barrier between "inside" and "outside" developed, giving rise to what Taylor calls the "buffered self." In contrast to the openness of being "porous," the buffered self doesn't believe there are things "out there" that can act through it. Everything "outside" of human minds must be seen as neutral, a blank canvas until human minds came along and saw it. This also took away the hierarchy of the ordered cosmos, the interrelation of all things. They no longer had their own place, no meaning that humans didn't impose on them. Taking away that independent meaning effectively "disenchanted" them.

So we ended up with a different model of the heavens, where the Earth became just another planet hanging in space. This "disenchanted universe" has a kind of order, too, but it is not the hierarchy of the enchanted cosmos. Things do what they do now because of impersonal mechanisms, laws of physics like gravity and magnetism, not because they have a pre-ordained place and inalterable role. Looking up isn't like looking into a cathedral anymore. The planets don't sing in their orbits. It's conceivable that we're looking up into a black, gaping void, and there's nothing meaningful, nothing independent, nothing else like us out there.

If there's nothing meaningful out there, then all the outside influences of the enchanted cosmos must be an illusion. They must come from somewhere inside the self. Think about Kit Walker's claims of abduction by "little green men"—to everyone else, these claims are another good reason to keep him in the *Asylum*. When Vivien can't rationally explain what's happening around her in "*Murder House:* Rubber Man," she thinks she must be hallucinating as a side-effect of her nausea medication. That the Blood Moon might affect conditions at *Roanoke* is initially dismissed as dumb superstition by most of the cast and crew. As things kick off in "*Roanoke:* Chapter Two," Matt says "I started to think that maybe I had suffered some sort of neurological damage . . . I secretly hoped that I had. At least that would have made sense." In the enchanted cosmos, the forces involved in these cases would be real, independent, outside things. But to the "buffered self" in the "disenchanted universe," they are just "inside" the mind.

Forces of evil aren't independent of the buffered self either. "The devil doesn't reside in Hell," declares the ex-Nazi physician, Arthur Arden, in "*Asylum:* Welcome to Briarcliff". "He lives right here in the frontal gyrus. The occipital lobes." And in "*Hotel:* Chutes and Ladders," the homicide detective John Lowe is certain that there's nothing else "out there" that can do evil. "I've worked every kind of crime. Robbery, homicide, assault," he insists. "Not one of them was committed by a ghoul or a ghost. People do enough damage without help from the afterlife."

In ways like these, all parts of the hierarchy of the ordered, enchanted cosmos are re-interpreted into something else. The buffered self "de-tunes" all these elements of reality, and no longer finds them anywhere. All those outside agencies become cases of superstition, madness, hallucination, and illusion. Everything meaningful is brought inside the cordons of the "buffered" Self.

Know Thy Self

So what would all this mean to anyone who found themselves in a Horror Story? Well, there are a few clear survival advantages to seeing oneself as a porous Self in an enchanted cosmos. Like somebody viewing *American Horror*

Story from the comfort of their couch, porous selves know beyond a doubt that the supernatural threats are real and deadly. They take them seriously, and act accordingly.

The long-term occupants of the *Hotel* are porous in this way. They don't piss off the vampiric Countess, and they're wary of the captive blood-starved Ramona. Even the Countess is afraid in "*Hotel:* Flicker" when another of the Hotel's secrets is let loose. Or take Edward Mordrake's visit to *Freak Show*. For Ethel and the other carnies, the story isn't silly superstition. It's reality. They try to avoid summoning the vengeful two-faced spirit by refusing to perform on Halloween. When he does appear, they follow his requests, laying bare their souls. Their honest compliance reveals to Mordrake that they aren't the twisted, corrupt souls he is looking for. It saves their lives.

In contrast, buffered Selves often put themselves in danger by assuming that their world is disenchanted. To them, only certain kinds of things exist, and only certain kinds of things can affect them. Despite their debt to disengaged rationality, buffered selves sometimes become too rigid to respond to events properly when things outside of that framework appear. They're reluctant to believe the evidence of their senses. So, it's Elsa Mars, so much "above" carnie superstition, who accidentally summons Mordrake to the *Freak Show*, and who ends up moments from becoming his victim when, in her pride, she fails to see him for what he is. We've seen how slow the occupants of the Roanoke and Murder Houses are to get out while they still can. When events in the disenchanted world don't seem to make sense, the buffered self is crippled with a paralyzing self-doubt. As the ghostly mass-murdering millionaire James Patrick March chides John Lowe in "*Hotel:* Devil's Night," "All you care about is evidence. . . . Until that evidence no longer fits the narrative you need to be true, at which point the evidence becomes an illusion, a mistake. A trick."

The idea of that trick can lead the buffered self to a very particular fate. "Gaslighting" is a word for describing the process of convincing a person to doubt their own sanity, or the evidence of their senses, as Hayden and the other ghosts do to Vivien in *Murder House*. Because Vivien refuses to believe her own suspicions, she stays passive far too long in the Murder House. In "*Asylum:* I am Anne Frank," Oliver Thredson, the real "Bloody Face," tries to gaslight Kit Walker into saying that he wasn't abducted, that he's responsible for Thredson's murders.

In the *Hotel*, Alex Lowe plays on her husband John's precarious state of mind to blind him to what's going on around him. She tries to convince him that things he experiences—his discovery of the sleeping chamber, the visit of the Swedish nymphomaniacs—are "all in his mind." Worse still, John's buffered self and his desperate need for control mean that he can't imagine how another person could act through him. If John believed his Self to be less impenetrable, less sacrosanct, he'd discover the Ten Commandments Killer's identity a bit sooner.

On the face of it, it seems like we might as well decide to be porous, just to be on the safe side. Unfortunately, it's not as simple as that. It ain't easy, being porous. With the change in attunement, reality might begin to disclose things we don't really want to see. In "*Murder House:* Piggy Piggy," Billie Dean Howard complains about the burden she took on when her murdered cleaning lady appeared to her ("Do you think I wanted a bloody Mexican ghost in my bathroom?"). Becoming porous would leave us devastatingly vulnerable to forces and pressures from outside our once-buffered selves, most of which we won't understand.

Think of the re-constituted Kyle in *Coven*, torn apart by all the conflicting impulses, memories and personalities that make up his composite body and mind. He's bewildered to the point of violence, even self-harm. And there's a real loss of control involved, too. Think of the relationship between John Lowe's Self, his sense of control, and his willingness to drink alcohol. Or the agony of (the real) Sister Mary Eunice, who pleads for release from the demon's clutches. You could even become porous and still fail to be properly prepared for the assault of the supernatural, as the disembowelment of

Cricket in "*Roanoke*: Chapter Four" graphically illustrates. The enchanted cosmos is full of dangerous forces. Deciding that they exist will only help us deal with them. It won't make us immune from them.

What's more, it would be very difficult to become truly porous today. A key feature of the enchanted cosmos was that its features were universally accepted. Faith in the existence of spirits wasn't a lifestyle choice, one option for belief among many others. They were "believed" in the same way that most people today "believe" the Earth is round. It was simply reality. Today, we're all aware that others might not agree with us if we start announcing the existence of the supernatural. As Taylor puts it, "each one of us as we grew up has had to take on the disciplines of disenchantment." This makes it too easy for us to spot superstition, mistakes, and even insanity in others.

True, being porous might protect us from mistakenly believing that we're being gaslighted, and thus help us get out of danger. But it could make things far worse if there really *is* some gaslighting going on, since acting porous in a disenchanted world might make everyone else think we're mad. Being seen as insane can be just the same as actually being insane. Dr. Thredson uses this trick repeatedly on Lana and Kit in the *Asylum,* relying on everyone seeing them only as psychiatric patients, as unreliable witnesses. So there is a social dimension to the reality we live in. We can't just "re-enchant" the human universe. We can't go back to being "naive."

Lessons for Self-Improvement

Does this mean we're doomed to being "buffered," no matter what? Not necessarily. Here are the survival lessons we can draw from all this:

First, avoid the blind rigidity of the buffered self, which assumes it can explain everything with disengaged rationality. Take a pragmatic approach to reality: essentially, this means "never having to say you're certain." As Taylor says, "what is real is what you have to deal with, what won't go away just because it doesn't fit with your prejudices." This should help you spot and avoid potential danger.

But second, don't invite danger by trying to becoming too porous. You may not be ready for what it lets in to your reality. And remember that we can't always rely on others to share that reality. The results of being porous when everyone around you is buffered could be just as dangerous as the blindness of being buffered on your own.

This leads us to the final measure we can take. An open mind could be matched with an open heart. At the end of every *American Horror Story*, after all the bone-saws have been blunted, the severed limbs carted off and the red stuff washed away, there's always some kind of community left. The Harmon and the Lowe families achieve greater happiness and mutual love in their (un)death than they were ever capable of in life.

Same for the less literal "families" of the *Freak Show* and the *Hotel*, united by trust, friendship, and shared experiences at the end of their tales. Kit Walker of the *Asylum*, and Jimmy, Dot, and Bette of the *Freak Show* are beginning new families as their stories draw to their end. The sisterhood of the *Coven* emerges through all its troubles stronger than ever before. Even the slaughter at *Roanoke* closes with a woman and child swearing to protect each other. Everyone in these communities shares a world, a reality with each other. They spread the risks and burdens of porousness among themselves, and they get rid of the dangers of disbelief among buffered selves by staying with like-minded (or "like-Selved") folks.

So, now that you understand the Self, the world that's tied to it, and the implications for being in a Horror Story, maybe the best thing to do is find someone else who could be in their own Horror Story, and pass along this guide.

5
Other People's Body Parts

CHARLENE ELSBY AND ROB LUZECKY

In *American Horror Story: Coven*, Kyle Spencer's reaction to his new (slightly used) body parts is to be expected, when we take into account how personal a body is to a person. Theories about how the body is related to a person's character abound in contemporary culture and also throughout the history of philosophy.

Physiognomy, for instance, has been around since early Greek medicine, and Aristotle refers to physiognomists in his works (especially the ones about animals and their parts). The basic question here is whether the body matters to a soul and, if it does, what is it about having the wrong body parts that causes it to suffer? Clearly, Kyle Spencer's new body doesn't seem to be working for him, but what exactly is wrong with just sewing together any old body parts that happen to fit?

The Body, the Soul, the Person, the Mind

We have words for "body," "soul," "person," and "mind," but it's not always clear how these all fit together, or whether there are in fact, four separate things. When we talk about a "person", we tend to think of individuals, whom we call by names. We may not know what the full metaphysical definition of "person" is, but we know that Madison Montgomery is one. But how do we define a "person"? By their mind, their soul, their body, or some mixture of these?

In *American Horror Story: Freak Show*, we might think we've found some examples of people who are on the borderline of personhood. After all, a person has one head, whereas Bette and Dot Tattler (with one body between them) have two heads (or they each have one). So does that make them two persons? Only if we define "person" according to something other than a body.

Bette and Dot have one body, except for the head part. Does that mean we can define a person as a head, such that for each head we have a person? Not really, because we don't look at severed heads and say that they're people. So it seems we're relying on something else in order to define what a person is, and it's not necessarily something bodily.

Bette and Dot have very different personalities, and neither one usually knows what the other one is thinking. But where is thought located? A range of answers exist in philosophy, and it's not important here to decide between them. Some philosophers (called reductive materialists) might say that a person is their body and only their body, in which case Bette and Dot are really just their brains (and two brains equals two people).

Other philosophers might say that the person is really a body plus something else that makes it unique—not just the brain, but the immaterial mind, so the person is a body and a mind somehow existing together. It seems that we can't just base our definition on a body, because then any variation to a body might exclude that person from the whole class of humanity, something which we try to avoid. If we say that a human person is a two-legged land mammal, then Elsa Mars wouldn't count. We would run into all sorts of conceptual difficulties, like, what is she? She used to be human, and then she lost her legs, so what is she now? How can you just switch species like that? It seems to make a whole lot less sense to claim that there aren't any one-legged people than it does to claim that a person is something other than a leg.

When you start talking about souls, things get a lot stickier, because "soul" is one of those words whose definition changes vastly depending on who's using the word and in what context. According to Aristotle, the soul is the *psyche* (where we get the word "psychology", even though psychologists now would use "mind" instead of "soul"). The soul is responsible for all of the faculties of a living thing. People have the most faculties, the main ones of which are growth, decay, nutrition, locomotion, perception and thought (this last one is what makes us human).

A soul and a body exist as one unified thing, as long as the person is alive. Other concepts of the soul aren't so naturalistic, though. Medieval philosophers who claim that the human soul has aspects of the divine will want to make it a separate thing from the body; it's something that exists with the body, sure, but to claim that the soul is responsible for digestion is blasphemy (they might say).

The debate surrounding the existence of the soul always comes down to whether it is separable from the body. People want to know if there's an afterlife or not. That is to say, does the soul outlive the body, or survive the body's death? If so, then it must be something related to the body but not the body itself. If the soul and the body were two aspects of a composite thing, as Aristotle tells us, then we might answer "No" to the afterlife question. If the soul and the body are together like the shape of a table and its wood, then when I chop up the table and burn it, its tableness doesn't just float safely away. It no longer exists. I destroyed it when I burned the wood. And so if the body and soul are inseparable, then the one dies with the other.

So what constitutes the destruction of the soul? To destroy something means to alter it in some significant way so that it no longer meets the definition for what it is supposed to be. If I want to destroy a table, I need only make it nonfunctional as a table. (Perhaps I chop it right down the middle, so that its surface is no longer able to hold things up off the floor, as any good table would.) To destroy the human soul, we might need only to destroy someone's capacity for thought—thought, after all, is what makes someone "human," according to Aristotle's definition (a "human" is a rational animal).

An animal is defined according its capacity to perceive; that is, any animal, to be considered an animal, must have some kind of perception. In order to exist, an animal must at the very least have the sense of touch, which is the most basic of the senses. If the sense of touch in an animal is destroyed, so is the animal. (When Madison is resurrected, she seems to have lost her ability to feel pain, which has to do with the sense of touch.) Take that idea along with the idea that any sense organ can be destroyed by perceiving something that is too extreme for it. We can be blinded by bright lights and deafened by loud noises. And that is why, on Aristotle's account, touching an animal too hard will kill it—it will overload its sense of touch, which is the faculty it needs to be defined as an animal (Aristotle, *De Anima* III.13) And when the animal dies, its faculty of perception goes right along with it. Just like the tableness in the table, it doesn't float off when the body is destroyed.

But if the body and soul are separable, there are a host of other problems that arise. If there are two separate things constituting my person, how and in what way are they connected? *Where* is my soul? What does it have to do with the body? Why is my soul in this body and not some other body, and why *this sort* of body?

The Body and Its Soul, the Soul and Its Body

Plato had an early theory of how the various body parts were formed. The explanations he advanced in *Timaeus* are based on a creation theory wherein particular body parts have particular purposes. We have vision, for instance, so that we can see the regular motions of the planetary bodies, become interested in astronomy, and then math, and then philosophy. So the reason we have eyes is that we're meant to study philosophy. Just like the gifts of the Supremes, body parts provide only the potential to act—and the same potential can be used for good or evil. It's the boring, everyday equivalent of being able to use your pyrokinesis for multiple ends; you could decide to use it to light your friends' cigarettes, or to set someone's curtains on fire.

Aristotle advances a similar but more naturalistic theory. All of our body parts are suited to particular purposes, and if we want to figure out why our back teeth are flat, we need only to look at what we're doing with them (grinding some food, probably). At a very basic level, things are suited to their environments; birds have parts suited to life in the air, sea creatures have parts suited to living in the sea, and land mammals have parts suitable for living on land.

Misty Day gets along well in the swamp, but she still can't breathe water; she's definitely a land mammal. And because the soul was also a natural phenomenon for Aristotle, the soul of the animal would be suited to its particular life as well. If an animal has wings, the soul is what makes them flap (or not); and if something has eyes, the soul is responsible for the fact that they see (as opposed to a disembodied eye which, according to Aristotle, isn't really an eye—eyes, after all, are eyes because they see things, and disembodied eyes don't).

These general theories about how the soul relates to the body provide a theoretical basis on which it is possible to surmise how a *particular* soul relates to a *particular* body. Starting way back with Plato, philosophers have tried to explain how the body relates to the soul not only in the general sense, but in any particular individual.

Plato, for instance, describes how a soul is reincarnated into a body best fitting its particular vices from a previous life (*Timaeus*). This is, in fact, where the rest of the animals came from. First men were created, and those who weren't morally perfect would come back in the bodies of women (on this account, women are basically just cowardly men). Aristotle goes on to specify how it is that women's bodies are demonstrably worse than men's. His explanation relies on the idea that any way in which a woman's body diverges from the form of a man's is to the woman's detriment. (We should all aim to be Greek men, according to dead old Greek men).

If someone were particularly flighty, on the other hand, they would come back as a bird. People whose interests were too earthly, who failed to realize that they should be studying philosophy instead of concerning themselves with material things, were condemned to have their legs taken away, so that they could be closer to the ground they so longed for (e.g., snakes). If you were a really terrible person, the kind who doesn't deserve to breathe air, you might come back as a fish. There's a fan theory about *American Horror Story* that follows the same reasoning—that the cast members from one season to the next are reincarnated as new characters fitted to their particular foibles.

When people try to correlate specific bodily characteristics with specific character traits, we call it physiognomy. The earliest book on the theory is probably Aristotle's *Physiognomonics*, although we should mention that it probably wasn't written by him. (It's questionable whether any of Aristotle's works were actually written by him; in general we attribute them to the school of Aristotle rather than claim that one guy wrote everything there was to know about logic, ethics, medicine, physics, genetics, and even how much wine an elephant can drink). It makes sense that an Aristotelian would hold a kind of physiognomy, given what he thinks about the soul (that it's a natural thing that animates a body). But some things he says are just odd, like when he claims that small people have small minds (*Physiognomonics*). Think of poor Ma Petite from the *Freak Show* season. Aristotle thinks her soul is tiny.

Over the history of philosophy, variations of the theory have reoccurred, and it's a matter of fact that people think they can judge other people just by looking at them. Despite how often we say that "You can't judge a book by its cover," the general consensus seems to be that the cover is a very good indication of what's inside the book. While we fault people now for judging someone based on their physical appearance, it's also how we might explain why Kyle doesn't take very kindly to his new physical form.

When Madison and Zoe set upon putting Kyle back together after the bus accident, they don't put him back together using his own parts. Instead, Madison tries to find the best bits, but the best bits in this case aren't the best for Kyle, who would much prefer his own parts. There are a lot of things we might like to change about ourselves, but, when pressed, a lot of people would prefer to keep their own body parts rather than literally trade them with someone else's. If I say I would like to have the abdominal muscles of some other person, it doesn't mean that I would like to cut the abs off of that person and replace my own with them. I would generally mean that I would like to work out my own abs hard enough for them to become similar to those other abs.

There are two main kinds of theory that might explain why we prefer our own body parts to other people's. The first sort of theory is that described by Ibn Sina in *The Salvation*. A lot of Medieval Philosophers, Ibn Sina included, used Aristotle's concepts as a basis on which they might propose their own theories. Ibn Sina proposed that what was properly the self wasn't the kind of soul Aristotle was describing, but a sort of nexus that held all of the soul faculties together. If the soul is responsible for all of movement, perception, and rational thought, there must be a nexus in addition that holds them all together. It would be like a pincushion that keeps a bunch of individual pins in place, or the bit of rope that holds a bundle together.

The soul comes into being and yearns for a particular kind of body, that which is suited to its particular purposes. If, for instance, your soul wanted to play piano very well, it might yearn for a body with longer fingers than most. How individual souls become united with individual bodies is kind of like how you might choose which vehicle to buy; if you move a lot, you might go for a truck rather than a sports car. According to this theory, the body is very much the soul's vehicle.

The body is like clothing; we put it on based on what seems fitting to wear that particular day. If we want to go hiking, we put on our hiking shoes and go; similarly, if the soul wants to be a great hiker, it would yearn for a body with a great capacity for walking around. We get used to our clothes, and we get used to our body, until eventually we think of them as a part of us, when in fact they are not. A theorist like Ibn Sina would say that Kyle Spencer's soul chose his body because it had a particular purpose in mind. To try to put him together using other people's body parts defies the soul's purpose. It would want to do things this body wasn't meant for; it's like trying to eat soup with a fork. This body simply won't do.

Another kind of theory uses the same concept of a habit in its explanation of the body, but without the dualistic concept of the soul. (A "dualist" conceives of the soul-mind and body as two separate and related things; in Ibn Sina's theory, the soul drives the body like an all-terrain vehicle.) Maurice Merleau-Ponty, in *The Phenomenology of Perception*, describes how a person's body is best defined by its capacity to act on the world, again, defined greatly by its particular attributes. The body is something habitual that is formed through the relation of a person with its world. When, after learning to work a doorknob and opening doors over and over again, I start to do it habitually, without even thinking; my hand has literally become a door-opening thing.

Merleau-Ponty even extends the theory to things we wouldn't think of as being part of the body. If something is used habitually towards our purposes, and we use it as if it were part of our body, it becomes a part of our body. So if the Axeman is constantly using his axe, and he uses it without even thinking about it like we might use our hands, then that axe becomes a part of his phenomenal body. It's like when you're used to carrying something around in your pocket and then notice that it's not there—something's off; you forgot your keys. The Axeman might notice that when he's not carrying his axe around, *his arm* feels a little too light. The axe has become a part of his habitual body, and not to have it makes the world seem not quite right. It's the same idea as the phantom limb phenomenon. When people lose a limb, they still have habitual ways of behaving that use the limb, and they may find themselves trying to do things with the missing limb, only to find themselves thwarted by their own bodies.

Kyle Spencer's reaction to his new body is completely comprehensible, when we consider how habitual our interactions with the world become. When I go to type, I do so with fingers of a certain length. If I were to put on some long, pointy fingernails and try to type as I usually would, it wouldn't work as well. I'd say that the new fingernails were getting in my way, even though they're pretty much my body parts.

Now Kyle Spencer is trying to walk around on someone else's legs. That's got to mess with you a little.

II

When bad things keep happening to good people, you start to question what is right and what is wrong

6
Horror Can Be Great Drama

S. EVAN KREIDER

American Horror Story does just what it says on the label, telling horrific Americana-flavored stories from season to season. We watch, enthralled by a cold fascination, as these grisly tales unfold.

But some of us watch with occasional pangs of uneasiness, or at least the feeling that we may be indulging a weakness. This is *horror*, and therefore by definition something not-serious, something possibly aimed at maladjusted teenagers with disordered emotional responses.

True, horror stories can be badly conceived and feeble, but so can any other kind of stories. If we look at *American Horror Story*, in particular the first two seasons, *Murder House* and *Asylum*, we can see that we're dealing with dramatic art at a high level, and furthermore dramatic art with important ethical lessons.

The standards for good drama, or good fiction, were laid down by Aristotle two and a half thousand years ago, and they still apply today. Many of today's Hollywood screenwriters will tell you that they didn't really understand what they were doing until they read Aristotle—okay, let's be honest, more likely someone's executive summary of Aristotle. If a promising new movie bombs, the critics' explanations of just what was wrong with it often sound as if they came straight out of Aristotle.

Aristotle wrote about what makes for good drama in his book *Poetics*. The title's misleading. Plays in the ancient world were generally in verse, and *Poetics* is really about drama, especially the kind of drama known as tragedy (which more or less means any kind of drama that doesn't aim primarily to get laughs).

Aristotle on What Makes for Good Tragedy

One of Aristotle's fundamental principles of tragedy is *mimesis*—meaning that drama imitates or represents human actions—not human actions which actually have occurred (that would be history, not drama) but human actions which we can imagine as having occurred.

American Horror Story clearly involves representations of human actions, as the various characters are depicted doing various things. It also fits nicely with Aristotle's notion of tragedy specifically in that it is serious rather than comic in tone; although there are moments of dark humor, the overall tone of the show avoids the campiness we find in some horror.

American Horror Story deals with possible actions rather than actual ones. "Possible" does not have to mean "realistic" in the sense of limiting itself to what we believe can take place in the real world. After all, we believe (hope?) that the various supernatural and paranormal elements that the show depicts (witches, aliens, and whatnot) don't in fact exist. However, "possible" needn't have such a strict interpretation, but can instead simply refer to imaginable events rather than factual ones, within the context of the story and its basic assumptions, which may include the supernatural and other things not of the real world.

Aristotle had no trouble describing the tragedies of his day as depicting "possible" human actions, despite the fact that they sometimes included supernatural elements such as the ancient Greek gods (which it is unlikely that Aristotle believed existed, considering his more monotheistic discussions of God in the *Metaphysics*).

Aristotle says that tragedy has six elements:

- ***plot***
- ***character***
- ***thought***
- ***style***
- ***lyrics (music)***
- ***spectacle (visual effects)***

These are not equally important. Plot is the most important, while a drama could even do without music or spectacle.

Plot is the situation in which the characters find themselves. It presents them with problems which they have to solve. The plot tiers the actions together into a coherent whole, so that the events played out are not just a succession of events or a meaningless jumble of unrelated actions.

Because it is the most important formal element of tragedy, Aristotle discusses plot more fully than the others. According to Aristotle, the plot should be complete; that is, it should involve a self-contained story with a clear beginning, middle, and end. That's not to say that a tragedy cannot rely on or make reference to general cultural knowledge or even other tragedies (after all *Oedipus Rex*, the kind of play Aristotle was thinking about, is part of a trilogy of tragedies), but it should be able to function as a self-standing whole that a viewer will be able to follow and derive a moral from even without that other knowledge.

Also, a plot should be of a certain magnitude; that is, neither the plot itself or the events it depicts should be too long or too short. Aristotle seems to have preferred tragedies that could be viewed as a whole in a single session, dealing with events that take place within a single, in-fiction day. However, if he were familiar with contemporary television series, he might not object to the multi-episode format depicting longer stretches of time, as long as they were appropriate to the story being told. Aristotle also notes that a plot may be simple or complex, the latter including reversal (a change in fortune, usually from good to bad) or recognition (a transition from ignorance to knowledge) for one or more of the dramatic personae.

Character means, not just a list of different people with names, but rather, individuals with definite moral character, so that they can be recognized by the way they act and the things they do.

Thought refers to the intentions, motives, virtues, and vices behind the actions, typically revealed through their speech.

Style is the rhythm and quality of the character's speeches. In Aristotle's time, like in Shakespeare's, this would usually be in the form of verse. Characters would speak in "lines" with a certain rhythmic pattern (or "meter") and sometimes rhyming.

Spectacle means all the visual elements of the play, everything the audience can see, such as props, costumes, and sets. This is the least important of the elements, because we can imagine and interpret the moral content from the play simply by reading it.

With regard to the six formal elements of tragedy, *American Horror Story* has the majority, including the most important ones. Certainly it has plot—indeed, most modern television shows do. *American Horror Story* also depicts the moral characters of the shows various personae, both heroes and villains, and does so not only through their actions, but also through their thoughts, revealed through the show's dialogue.

The show lacks "style" as Aristotle defines it, since the characters do not speak with poetic rhyme and rhythm, though we could certainly imagine them doing so if the writers had so chosen (*Shakespearean Horror Story*?). But it does have style in the sense that sentences spoken have a particular rhythmic quality which influences how we understand them.

The show mostly lacks "lyrics" as Aristotle defines them, since the characters do not typically burst out into song

(*American Horror Musical*?), though *Freak Show* proves the primary exception, depicting as it does Elsa Mars opening each night with a musical number. If we interpret lyrics more broadly to include the show's soundtrack, then perhaps we could say that they all contain this formal element, especially *Coven*, which makes very good use of Fleetwood Mac (including a guest appearance by the white witch herself, Stevie Nicks).

In any case, Aristotle feels that style and lyrics are optional, and would not criticize the show if it lacked them. Finally, *American Horror Story* does feature spectacle. Obviously, this includes all of the usual: sets, makeup, costumes, and props. More specifically, the show contains the kind of spectacle appropriate to the horror genre, which includes some blood and guts and other gore, though to varying degrees: *Murder House* is probably on the lesser side of the blood and guts meter, while *Coven* and *Hotel* are quite a bit more graphic on occasion.

However, *American Horror Story* does not rely purely on gory effects for cheap scares, but rather uses these effects as a means to more chilling psychological effect. In that way, it has less in common with so-called "torture porn" or "splatter fest" horror, and more in common with psychological horror such as Hitchcock's movies. Ultimately, we could imagine finding *American Horror Story* just as chilling if we were reading a novelization rather than watching the show, and in that way, it makes use of spectacle in a way of which Aristotle would approve.

Aristotle claims that the plot should be of a certain magnitude and complete. This suggests that Aristotle might not be fond of most modern television series, many of which have long seasons of about two dozen episodes spread out over several months, sometimes including long breaks for holidays. Aristotle would likely think that this made them of an overly large magnitude, breaking up the moral and psychological effects, so that it's too difficult for the audience to follow and absorb the story. Also, television series tend not to be complete within each season, but only over the course of the whole series, if even then. This risks leaving story lines and characters undeveloped.

However, Aristotle would probably think more highly of *American Horry Story* with regard to both its completeness and magnitude. First, it has shorter seasons, with ten to thirteen episodes, and breaks kept few and short. Second, each season tells an independent, self-contained story, focusing on different events with different personae. True, there are occasional inter-season references; for example, *Hotel* has a brief guest appearance by one of the witches from *Coven*. However, the audience need not have seen *Coven* to understand what is happening in *Hotel*; the reference is merely an "Easter egg" for fans who have followed multiple seasons of the show.

Aristotle would also characterize *American Horror Story* as having complex plots, in that they involve reversal and recognition. The latter features less prominently, though there are still occasions of characters moving from ignorance to knowledge. However, the real strength of *American Horror Story* lies in its clever use of reversal, sometimes even involving a double-reversal: a character may move from good fortune to bad fortune, then back to good again.

In *Murder House*, there are certainly moments of recognition, such as when Ben and Vivien discover that their daughter Violet had died and that they had been interacting with her ghost. However, more interesting is the double reversal that Ben experiences, moving from happy family man, to head of a near-broken household, then back to happy family man (though only in death). For another example, in *Asylum*, a key moment of recognition is when Sister Jude realizes that Sister Mary Eunice has changed from a meek minion to a sadistic tyrant (in fact, possessed by the Devil). However, this is just a catalyst for Sister Jude's reversals, from Mother Superior, to asylum patient, then to free woman.

Catharsis and the Role of Fear and Pity

According to Aristotle, the purpose of tragedy is to arouse fear and pity, and to bring about a *catharsis* of these emotions—a profound experience which changes us. Aristotle does not say much about the nature of this catharsis, and its exact meaning is up for debate.

Traditionally, catharsis has been interpreted as a "purging" of emotions, an opportunity simply to rid oneself of them. More recently, some scholars have argued that Aristotle's intent was to describe something more like a "purification" or "perfecting" of these emotions, a way of practicing them in the safe, virtual context of tragedy so that we can express them in real life in an appropriately virtuous manner. This later interpretation has the benefit of cohering nicely with some of Aristotle's other ideas about morality and virtue, furthermore, it fits very nicely with the moral tone of *American Horror Story*, as we shall see.

Generally speaking, Aristotle believes that tragedy should show people with relatable moral characters—that is, not perfectly good, but not thoroughly evil either. It should also depict them experiencing a reversal of fortune—specifically, from good fortune to bad fortune—as a logical result of their own behavior.

A key concept here is *hamartia*, traditionally thought of as a "tragic flaw," but more generally, as connoting errors of judgment and mistaken actions, sometimes through a lack of moral character, but also through simple ignorance. By presenting relatable characters who suffer the ill effects of their moral mistakes, Aristotle believes tragedy can teach the audience about right action and virtuous character.

The relatability of character is especially important to arousing the audience's fear and pity. We can only feel fear for characters with whom we can relate, so they must be generally decent but not perfect people—presumably just like us. We also cannot feel pity for thoroughly evil people, as pity requires some sense that the person suffering does not deserve the suffering to the same degree that evil people do. Thus, good-but-not-perfect moral character is the best for fulfilling the purpose of catharsis. Furthermore, these are best effected by way of the plot rather than mere spectacle. For example, gross special effects create only very shallow, temporary feelings of fear and pity, whereas the plot communicates deeper and more lasting effects.

With all this in mind, it's likely that Aristotle would have thought well of *Murder House*. Indeed, the season fits the mold of a classical tragedy very well. Ben strikes the audience as a generally decent fellow, but one suffering from the tragic flaw of lust, which leads to his infidelity. After that, he seems swept up in events that follow, including the murder of his lover, and the subsequent attempt to keep both the infidelity and murder from his wife and daughter. As Aristotle might have said, Ben is a good but flawed person who suffers from a result of his own actions, but perhaps disproportionately to them, making it easy for us to identify with, fear for, and pity him.

We also see the tragic results stemming from his flawed actions, the ultimate death of himself and his family. As such, this offers a clear moral message for the audience about the severe consequences of infidelity. However, *Murder House* goes a step further than the average classical tragedy by offering the second reversal, in which the family's ghosts are reunited in death. Ben, having suffered enough for his misdeeds, is now forgiven by his wife and daughter, and they are rewarded with a new (after)life in which they can be happy together. This offers the audience the additional moral message of the possibility of redemption.

Aristotle would also likely have thought well of *Asylum*, and for similar reasons. Sister Jude, though certainly a harsh Mother Superior, is still relatable, especially once her backstory is revealed. She became a nun after having accidently killed someone in a drunk-driving accident, and saw the event as God telling her to forsake her sinfully hedonistic lifestyle as an entertainer and to devote her life to fighting evil, especially that which she believes conceals itself as mental illness.

In her case, we might see *hamartia* as a simple mistake (the car accident) or as a tragic flaw (her harsh over-zealousness), but in either case, it leads her to a reversal, from Mother Superior to asylum patient. During her internment, she suffers from a number of pains and indignities, not the least of which is some severe shock therapy. Just as with Ben in *Murder House*, because we can identify with the goodness in Sister Jude, even with all her flaws, and because her suffering seems not entirely deserved, we can feel fear and pity for her, and take to heart the moral lessons that the story imparts—perhaps most obviously, "Pride comes before a fall."

Also like Ben, Sister Jude undergoes a second reversal, in which she is eventually released from the asylum, and comes to terms with her past, ultimately living and dying in peace; once again providing the audience with the moral message of the possibility of redemption.

Aristotle might not have thought as well of some other seasons of *American Horror Story*, as they seem not to fit quite as well with his ideas about tragedy. For example, it's not clear that *Coven* has a protagonist who compares as well for Ben or Sister Jude. Certainly Fiona (the Coven's Supreme Witch) and Cordelia (Fiona's daughter) both experience reversals: Fiona goes from a life as head of the Coven to an afterlife in hell, while Cordelia goes from terrorized and inadequate daughter to the new Supreme. However, Fiona, though surely not a two-dimensional villain, is not really a good enough person with whom we can identify, much less feel pity for, and her post-death punishment seems apt enough.

Similarly, Cordelia comes to a better end, but seems not to fit the mold of the tragic hero in the first place, her only real mistake being born to Fiona. One could argue something similar about Elsa Mars in *Freak Show*, whose heaven-like afterlife as the star of her eternal show seems undeserved, or many of the ghosts in *Hotel*, who finally end up happy, but who also seem not to deserve it, considering they spent so much of their afterlives torturing, terrorizing, and murdering hotel guests. All this makes the moral of these seasons a bit more muddled from Aristotle's perspective.

Virtue, Justice, and Redemption

Aristotle does touch on the relationship of tragedy to moral virtue in the *Poetics*, but a fuller grasp of the importance of this connection requires more details about his ideas on moral virtue, especially as presented in his main book on ethics, the *Nicomachean Ethics*. In *Nicomachean Ethics*, Aristotle characterizes a moral virtue as a mean between extremes: courage is the mean between cowardice and recklessness, generosity is the mean between extravagance and stinginess, and so forth.

Essentially, there is an appropriate range of human feeling and behavior that strives to avoid excesses; "all things in moderation," as the saying goes. Since people are not born perfectly virtuous, upbringing, and education are essential in training people to be virtuous. A system of rewards and punishments also contributes to this, whether it be in the form of a parent disciplining a child, or a society imposing legal sanctions on a criminal. And so, a detailed notion of justice is required for moral virtue. Unfortunately, Aristotle's discussion of justice is not as clear as we might like, as he seems to discuss a number of different kinds of justice, often without coming to a definitive conclusion about any one or the other. However, there are some aspects of justice that seem clear enough to apply here.

One is that justice can serve a retributive role; that is, treating people as they deserve to be treated, and correcting for that which is undeserved. For example, Aristotle discusses various ways in which justice can be applied to unfair or unequal economic transactions or social distributions, perhaps correcting for the vice of greed, and imposing a more generous outcome to the situation. This is also related to the idea of holding people responsible for their actions, something Aristotle applies to his discussion of voluntary behavior; when people voluntarily behave in an unvirtuous manner, we hold them responsible by punishing them for it. At the end of the day, good people deserve good things, and bad people deserve bad things.

This also suggests a rehabilitative role of justice, especially through punishment. Aristotle's notion of virtue involves more than simply doing the right thing, but also actively wanting to do the right thing. The virtuous person takes pleasure in behaving virtuously, and feels pain when acting viciously; whereas the vicious person takes pleasure in vicious acts, and fails to enjoy virtuous ones. Upbringing, education, and the legal system can help train people to be virtuous by helping them associate pleasure with virtue and pain with vice. The most obvious way to do this is through a system of rewards and punishments, and a just system of rewards and punishments will be sure to reward virtue and punish vice.

At the beginning of the *Murder House* season, we see that Ben lacks temperance, the virtue associated with pleasures of the flesh, and this has led him into temptation, culminating in an extra-marital affair with a young woman. When he decides to break it off, it is more from self-interest than virtue. Thus, he still lacks temperance, as demonstrated by his struggles with temptation by their housekeeper Moira, who appears to Ben as young, beautiful, and highly sexualized.

As the season progresses, Ben suffers various ills, including the loss of his daughter; but more importantly, he begins to take his share of the responsibility for these events, genuinely desiring to be a better person. Once he does so, he finally sees Moira in her true form, matronly and conservative, and Moira's own behavior toward Ben changes from one of temptation to one of support. Once Ben is reunited with his family in death, we see him finally content, genuinely taking pleasure in the virtuous behavior associated with a loving family; Moira in turn serves the family and protects them from the less virtuous ghosts in the house, especially the sociopathic Tate, who had become obsessed with Ben's family, especially his daughter Violet. In Ben's case, justice played the role not only of just deserts, but also as rehabilitation to virtue, even if this does not fully take hold until the afterlife.

This also applies nicely to *Asylum*. Sister Jude, despite her good intentions, clearly suffers from a lack of virtue. In Aristotle's terminology, we might say that she lacks "good temper" and suffers from "irascibility"; that is, she is too angry, even lapsing into cruelty on occasion. She also suffers from an overabundance of pride, thinking herself morally superior to her patients, not to mention Sister Mary Eunice. As a result, she routinely engages in vicious behavior towards those around her, terrorizing and severely punishing them on a regular basis.

After she is usurped and becomes a patient herself, she suffers justice as retribution, "an eye for an eye" treatment at the hands of Sister Mary Eunice and the rest of the staff. This treatment serves the rehabilitative role of allowing her to understand the unnecessary suffering she has caused to others. As a result, she learns to let go of her pride and anger, and becomes more virtuous.

By the time the season ends, we see that she has come to terms with her past behavior, both before and during her time as Mother Superior. She can forgive herself because she has suffered commensurately for her sins, but more importantly, because she has become a better person. Because of this, she meets a good end, dying peacefully among those who care for her.

Aristotle might take issue with other seasons of *American Horror Story*. In *Coven*, Fiona certainly suffers for her crimes, but does not really learn much from her punishments, failing to become more virtuous. In *Freak Show*, Elsa receives the reward of a happy afterlife, but without really having earned it. In *Hotel*, it's unclear whether we're supposed to think that the ghosts have really suffered for their vicious behaviors, especially since they enjoy them so much; worse, they receive a kind of "redemption" without having fully experienced justice first. Aristotle would likely have judged these seasons as morally inferior, since the message of virtue is murky at best, entirely missing at worst.

The Virtues of Horror

The horror genre gets a lot of criticism, some simply seeing it as inferior to other forms of drama, others even arguing that it contributes to immorality by desensitizing people to violence, if not encouraging actual violent behavior itself. However, it's clear that at least some horror can constitute legitimate works of art, and even teach us something about virtue, justice, and redemption.

These works actually have the power to make us better people. *American Horror Story* is just such a work.

7
And the Most Despicable Jessica Lange Character Is . . .

RACHEL ROBISON-GREENE

I think you'd be hard pressed to find an *American Horror Story* fan who doesn't miss the presence of Jessica Lange on the show. Lady Gaga certainly brought her own sizzle, but Lange provided the seasons she led with a gravitas that few others could offer. She brought complexity and humanity to some of the most despicable characters on television. Not a single one of them is without *severe* moral blemishes, but some of them are worse than others.

Philosophers through the years have had much to say about morality and the development of virtuous moral character. Clearly, none of Jessica Lange's characters have read any of those philosophers. The other day, I was reflecting on these seedy characters and the terrible things they've done. I found myself thinking, "Sure, all of Lange's characters are bad in some way or another, but which one is the *worst?*" You might have your own ideas about this. Join me as I bring some moral philosophy in to help me rank Lange's characters from bad to worst.

#4: Sister Jude

Sister Jude is Lange's most morally upright character. All right, she had reason to believe that she killed a little girl in a drunken hit and run and never reported it. She also enjoys exacting corporal punishment on people who are mentally ill. What's more, to punish Kit and Grace for fornicating in the kitchen she orders the asylum doctors to perform a surgery on Grace so that she can't have children. She has Lana Winters institutionalized even though she knew full well that Lana was perfectly sane. Those things are all really bad. But they aren't as bad as some of the actions that Lange's other characters perform.

Many moral philosophers believe that intentions determine the moral acceptability of actions. Immanuel Kant is perhaps the most famous philosopher to hold this view. According to this kind of moral theory, it's not enough to simply perform actions with good consequences. In order for an action to count as a moral action, you must perform it because you recognize that it's what you ought to do—it's your duty.

Imagine, for example, two different real estate agents, both trying to interest you in purchasing the Murder House. One agent discloses the house's dark past to you because she's concerned about what might happen to her if she doesn't (you might later sue her or otherwise ruin her career and reputation). The other agent discloses the information to you because she recognizes that disclosure to be the action that moral duty requires and her intention is to always do her moral duty. If Kant were living today and was a horror fan, he'd be sure to categorize the second agent's action as morally commendable. Even though the first agent performed the *very same action*, her action is not a moral action because of the nature of the intentions behind it.

On this card, I think that Sister Jude scores *some* points. We learn early on that when she was younger, Jude was an alcoholic torch singer who performed at dive bars where she enjoyed meeting up with random strangers and going home with them to enjoy a little after party. She hits rock bottom when she drives drunk and hits a little girl. After this incident, she decides to reform her life. She becomes a nun and, rather quickly, she is the Monsignor's right-hand woman.

Where Sister Jude parts ways with some of Lange's other characters on *American Horror Story* is that she actually cares about reforming her life. She cares, at least to some degree, about becoming a better person; she cares about determining what duty requires and then doing that thing. Of course, that sense of duty doesn't extend to actually turning herself in for the hit and run, but it's something. Like I said, she scores *some* points.

Jude also attempts to do her duty when she has reason to believe that Dr. Arden, the asylum doctor, is actually a Nazi war criminal. You'll recall that a woman claiming to be Anne Frank is brought to the asylum. When she sees Dr. Arden, she recognizes him instantly as one of the doctors who performed horrific experiments on Holocaust victims in concentration camps during the war. This seems to trouble Jude deeply. At great personal cost to herself and her advancement prospects, Jude reports her suspicions to the Monsignor. He advises her to promptly drop the issue. We learn later that the Monsignor was aware, at least to some degree, of Dr. Arden's unsavory research interests. Early in the relationship, he granted Dr. Arden permission to perform experiments on human subjects "for the greater good." Jude finds herself unable to let the matter go and she reports the issue to her Mother Superior, who commends Jude for her "moral compass." At the Mother's recommendation, Jude brings the matter to Nazi hunter Sam Goodman. Though the woman claiming to be Anne Frank turns out to be a woman suffering from severe post-partum depression, her obsession with the atrocities of World War II generated a true belief about the real identity of Dr. Arden. He is Nazi Doctor Hans Gruper.

The actions that Jude took in this case took great moral courage. It's true, of course, that Jude hates Dr. Arden and would welcome his removal from Briarcliff. But she also has very good reason to be *terrified* of Dr. Arden, knowing full well the kind of monster that he is and what he is capable of. She viewed her duty to bring his atrocities to light as more important than her own safety, which is one of the reasons she has my vote for the least despicable of Jessica Lange's *American Horror Story* characters.

Sister Jude also seems to experience an appropriate range of moral emotions. Many philosophers argue that our moral practices depend on emotions like approval, disapproval, guilt, shame, remorse, pride, gratitude, and so on. When we hold someone morally responsible for something—when we judge that they have done something wrong—we also think that it is appropriate for them to feel shame or guilt for their bad behavior. Think, for a moment about the worst moral agents imaginable—serial killers. One of the most frightening things about the world's worst serial killers is that they don't seem to experience any of these emotions in cases in which they clearly should. Twisty, and his homicidal heir apparent, Dandy, don't seem to experience any remorse whatsoever for the suffering and death that they cause.

Jude seems to agonize over the death of the child that she believes she killed. She clearly feels deep remorse for her actions. The memory drives her to drink, even all of these years later. Late in the season, her remorse compels her to go to the home of the parents of the girl she believed that she killed, presumably to confess what she had done. As it turns out, however, though she didn't imagine that she hit the girl in the road, the child did not die. While Jude sits on the couch, the hit and run victim walks into her parents' home as a fully-grown woman, dressed in a nurse's outfit. The parents express violent frustration with the unknown stranger who struck their child, breaking several of her bones. After hearing this, Sister Jude stops short of confessing her involvement.

She also clearly has strong sisterly or even maternal feelings toward Sister Mary Eunice, protecting her at many turns even after Mary Eunice is possessed by the Devil and behaving strangely.

She also experiences appropriate moral emotions after she is herself made a patient at the asylum. She now empathizes with at least some of the patients and she even apologizes to Lana Winters. Remorse is not a sentiment that we see often, if at all, in Lange's other characters.

I want to be careful not to overstate the case here. Sister Jude is not a *great* person. She runs her asylum with an iron fist. The patients in her care are mentally ill and deserve to be treated with kindness and compassion. Sister Jude seems, in the first half of the season, to be incapable of empathizing with the patients. It's only after she has been admitted as a patient herself that she gains some understanding of what people in that position go through and she begins to make progress.

#3: Elsa Mars

Right out of the gate you must have known that a character who dresses in a powder blue suit and performs a surreal rendition of David Bowie's *Life on Mars* couldn't possibly rank as Lange's most despicable. She's no saint either.

Elsa Mars, you'll recall, runs the freak show. She traveled the world finding performers for her show. In fact, in the season premiere, we witness her acquisition of the Siamese twins Dot and Bette. She's fond of telling her performers that some people are born into families, but her family was created. Elsa serves as the matriarch of the family that she brought together. To a certain degree, she takes responsibility for the group, viewing the continued survival of the show as her personal responsibility.

Some philosophers, many of whom call themselves *care ethicists*, argue that our moral obligations arise out of the set of roles and relationships that we choose for ourselves. The paradigm case of a role of this type is the role of a parent. When we choose to become parents, we take on a set of obligations to our children. The set of obligations that we take on when we become parents is different from the set we take on when we become spouses, when we take on jobs, or when we run for office. The exact nature of the set of obligations depends on the kind of role you are taking on.

Elsa takes her rule as matriarch of the freak show seriously and she seems to genuinely understand that the role she has taken on saddles her with certain moral obligations.

Despite the fact that she understands her role as a matriarch, she's very easily tempted to disregard that role, especially when fame is on the line. Many philosophers, including Aristotle, argue that being a virtuous agent is not about the way you behave in any single circumstance. Rather, virtue is demonstrated in the ways that we routinely, habitually behave. Recognizing that a moral obligation exists is not enough. A person is virtuous to the extent that they routinely satisfy those obligations. What's more, according to Aristotle, moderation is key to virtue. Elsa is powerless against the temptation to pursue fame and fortune. She isn't interested in a moderate degree of fame or success. She brought Dot and Bette into the freak show family because she believed doing so would revive the dying business. But when she realizes that, in addition to being oddities, the twins have talent and that the total package might upstage her own, she sells the twins to the overindulged, overgrown Dandy Mott, who later turns out to be a serial killer.

It might be necessary to take some mitigating factors into account in Elsa's case. Earlier in her life Elsa was a dominatrix and a prostitute. She was kidnapped and forced to participate in a snuff movie during which her legs were amputated. Her status as a person without legs is what attracted her to freak shows in the first place.

When tragedies like this happen to a person, we might want to cut them *some* slack. But not much.

#2 Constance Langdon

We meet Constance Langdon in the Murder House. She is the earliest of Jessica Lange's *American Horror Story* characters. I'm sure none of us really knew what to expect. As background details continued to unfold throughout the duration of the season, it became more and more clear just how despicable Constance Langdon really was. We learn that she is obsessed with physical beauty (this is true of more than one of Lange's characters). Constance is beautiful on the outside, but truly ugly on the inside. She is horrified when each of her three children turns out, in her view, to be ugly in various ways.

We said that Elsa Mars at least recognized the nature of her maternal obligations to the family that she created. Constance takes these role-based duties even less seriously than Elsa does. She is mortified by the ugliness that she sees in her children and is responsible, ultimately, in one way or another, for the deaths of all of them.

Some of the worst behavior Constance exhibits involves the way that she treats her daughter, Addy, who has Down syndrome. When Addy misbehaves, or gets in the way of something Constance wants to do, she locks her in the closet. Addy looks at the "pretty girls" in magazines and wonders aloud why she does not look like them. She tells her mother that she wants to dress up as a pretty girl for Halloween. Constance insists that Addy is *not* a pretty girl, and that it would be humiliating for her to dress up as one. Finally Constance lets her trick-or-treat as a "pretty girl," but only if she wears a vinyl mask. Rushing out into the street to show Violet her mask, Addy is hit by a car and dies.

This is the last of Constance's children to die. Her most beloved child was Tate, played by the handsome Evan Peters—the only child that Constance is proud of because he's the only one she views as physically attractive. Tate is truly a villain we love to hate. He is the maestro of the Murder House—arguably the most evil person in it. We learn that, though Tate is beautiful on the outside, he is hideous on the inside just like his mother. His final act as a living person was to commit a mass murder at his high school and then commit suicide by cop.

Constance's role in the death of her son Beauregard is more direct. Beau has craniodiaphyseal dysplasia, which leaves him physically deformed. He also has a mental disability. Out of embarrassment, Constance keeps Beau in the attic, chained to the bed. When Constance learns that she is being investigated for child neglect, she can't bear the idea of her son being taken away from her to be raised by the system, despite her shame in his outward appearance. Instead she asks her boyfriend, Larry Harvey, to smother Beau with a pillow. Larry goes through with it, and Beau becomes the Murder House's ghostly attic inhabitant.

Finally, we learn that Constance herself has committed murder rather than merely demanding others to kill for her. A flashback reveals that Constance walked in on Moira being raped by Constance's husband, Hugo. Constance promptly shoots them both.

Constance is as murderous or more so than any of the characters that Lange portrays. She is horribly emotionally abusive to her children and to other characters on the show (in one scene, she cooks a batch of cupcakes for Violet, dumps ipecac in them, and advises her daughter Addy to spit in the batter).

As troubling as all of this behavior may be, Constance does display some appropriate moral emotions, though certainly not at *all* the right times. She's genuinely grief-stricken at the death of her daughter, Addy. She seems to gain some perspectives on her life and desperately misses her children when they are all dead. There is at least *something* redeeming going on there.

#1 Fiona Goode

Coven Supreme Fiona Goode gets my vote for Lange's most despicable character. Many philosophers believe that moral actions necessarily involve considerations about *other people.* There isn't universal agreement on this topic, but it is a commonly held position that an action performed purely out of self-interest is not truly a moral action. If moral actions are actions that show concern for others rather than purely concern for the self, then Fiona Goode never behaves morally.

Fiona is the Supreme of the Coven, and the Coven should function like family. Again, we see Jessica Lange cast as the matriarch. The cast of characters that Lange plays is a study in the ways in which matriarchs can be moral failures. Early in the season, we learn that when a new Supreme is ascending, the old Supreme begins to grow weak. When Fiona's predecessor, Anne Leigh, began to grow weak and it was clear that Fiona would be her successor, Fiona slit Anne Leigh's throat. She wanted the greatest amount of power possible for the greatest amount of time possible.

There's room for only one Supreme, so when a new one starts to rise, that means death for the previous Supreme. As the series begins, Fiona is actively combating changes she is noticing in herself. The first time we encounter the character, she is talking to a doctor at a research facility about an experimental procedure that will make her young again.

In this respect, Fiona is a familiar character. She is an aesthete in the vein of Dorian Gray. For years her power as Supreme has shielded her from aging, disease, or decay. She could commit bad acts with impunity, while her outward appearance is the very picture of perfection.

We make value judgments every day—judgments about what things are good and bad and what things are right and wrong. Some value judgments are about beauty rather than morality. We're motivated by the set of things that we judge to be valuable. Most people are motivated by a combination of values. We listen to certain kinds of music or hang pieces of art on our wall because we find them beautiful. We treat our neighbors with kindness because we judge it to be the right thing to do.

But when characters in pop culture are motivated *exclusively* by aesthetic concerns, and when, on top of that, those aesthetic concerns seem entirely self-directed, a villain of a very particular type emerges. We are introduced to this character early in our childhoods through characters like the Evil Queen in *Snow White*. Fiona cares about looks and power above anything and anyone else.

The changes to her looks are not the only changes that she has noticed. She also recognizes that she's beginning to grow weak. She realizes that her tenure as Supreme is about to come to an end and she will do whatever she can to stop that from happening, up to and including killing the young girls in her coven to prevent them from taking her place.

You might think that, even if Fiona can't satisfy her obligations to her Coven family, she might have some inclination to satisfy obligations to her family by *blood.* If you thought that, you'd be wrong. Fiona is just about as cruel to her own daughter, Cordelia, as it's possible to be. She abandoned her as a baby in order to pursue a life of carnal pleasures. When she returned later in Cordelia's life, she subjected her to constant criticism and withheld maternal love.

All of Lange's characters do bad things. Fiona doesn't seem to have a moral bone in her body, and for that reason, she's my pick for most despicable Jessica Lange character on *American Horror Story*.

8
Night of the Living Disabled

MATTHEW WILLIAM BRAKE

In *American Horror Story: Murder House*, we first meet Adelaide "Addy" Langdon in 1978. She's a young girl with Down syndrome warning two twin boys to stay out of the Murder House. The twin boys, Troy and Bryan, ignore her advice and enter the Murder House. As they step inside, Addy gives an ominous warning, "You're gonna die in there" ("Pilot").

Flashing forward to 2011, Addy lives with her mother Constance next door to the Murder House in which the new neighbors, the Harmons, have just moved in. While Addy's unwelcomed intrusions into the Harmons' home are inappropriate, we feel a great deal of compassion for Addy on account from her mother's unceasing verbal abuse of her, calling Addy a "mongoloid" and a "monster." Thus, Addy struggles with issues of self-image, partly based on the abuse from her mother and partly based on the representations of women on different magazine covers about which she asks her mother, "How come I don't look like these girls?" ("Home Invasion"). Addy later tells her mother that she wants to be a "pretty girl," but her mother responds by saying that she will never be pretty ("Halloween, Pt. 1").

You'd be forgiven for assuming at the outset that Addy is a sinister, demonic figure and that she was responsible for the deaths of the twins. This recalls a common belief of the medieval and classical ages that disability was a sign of supernatural power or insight, and the opening scene seems to be playing around with that idea. However, it becomes obvious that this is not the case. As Addy's story unfolds, we learn that while she does indeed have many relationships with the ghosts who live in Murder House, she is just a sweet girl who is emotionally abused by her mother.

Eugenics, Disability, and Horror

Disability has a complex history with the horror genre. It certainly draws on ancient beliefs, but the modern horror genre is rooted in the eugenics era in the US. In her book, *Hideous Progeny*, Angela Smith quotes from a letter dated December 1931 from Colonel Jason S. Joy, administrator of Hollywood's Production Code, to an executive at Paramount regarding the forthcoming movie, *Dr. Jekyll and Mr. Hyde*. Smith wondered whether audiences were ready for the depiction of such a grotesque figure as Mr. Hyde to be portrayed on the big screen. We can see three eugenic assumptions in Colonel Joy's inquiry:

1. **The assumption that outward bodily differences are proof of inner aberrations.**
2. **The assumption that normal people naturally react negatively to seeing disability; thus, the disabled are self-evidently bad and could cause national harm.**
3. **The affirmation of the eugenic imperative to protect America by identifying the defective body, corralling it, and possibly disposing of it.**

In fact, eugenic propaganda films acted as a precursor to the modern horror genre in cinema, which emerged just as explicit eugenic medical films were coming under increasing scrutiny.

Smith mentions a number of eugenic films from between the years 1912 and 1927, specifically highlighting a movie entitled *The Black Stork*. It was produced with the express purpose of encouraging parents to allow infants with disabilities to die.

The movie depicts a couple who marry despite the advice of their doctor who informs them that the husband, Claude, carries a genetic defect. The couple conceives, and indeed, the child is born disabled. As the parents decide what to do and the doctor recommends that the child be allowed to die, the film attempts to show how terrible a life with disability can be, connecting disabilities to poverty and crime while also resorting to racial language to explain the child's genetic defects. In the end, the parents allow the child to die, and its soul is depicted as going to heaven to be with Jesus.

Constance, Addy, and Eugenic Logic

That *American Horror Story* should begin its first arc with disability playing an important role in the lives of some of the main characters is a testament to the creators' knowledge about the tropes and history of the genre as well as the depictions of disability in history.

The eugenic mentality is obvious in Constance, who wants to hide Addy from public view. During Halloween, Constance yells at Addy: "Do you know what they think when we walk down the street? 'There but for the grace of God go I'. You make them feel lucky. And they think I'm a hero, as though I've had some choice!" ("Halloween, Pt. 1"). As a form of punishment, Constance even locks Addy in a room full of mirrors or "the bad girl room" to look at herself, locking the door as Addy screams inside ("Home Invasion"). Constance's implicit eugenic thinking comes out further in a conversation with Vivian, who suspects that there's something wrong with her own child *in utero*:

> **VIVIAN:** Can I ask you a personal question? If you had known about Addy before she was born, would you have done something? When I first met you, you said that if they had had the tests back then that you might have . . .

> **Constance:** Oh, don't think I didn't think about it, even after she was born, leaving that little bug-eye out in the cold. That's what they do in China. ("Home Invasion")

While we may be horrified by Constance's attitude and language, even in our own world the threat of death and annihilation is never far from discourses about people with disabilities, whether in conversations about selective abortion or "death with dignity." The implicit assumption seems to be that it is better to be dead than to have a disability.

We see this logic come out explicitly after Addy is hit by a car and killed on Halloween night. For all the verbal abuse she heaped on Addy, Constance is heartbroken especially after she is unable to drag Addy's body to the Murder House property in time for her ghost to remain there. Constance is later able to communicate with Addy through a medium friend. Constance apologizes to Addy, and Addy informs her that "where she is now, on the other side, she's a pretty girl at last" ("Piggy, Piggy"). While this seems touching at first, further reflection makes me wonder how much different this really is from a movie like *The Black Stork*. Addy is only able to find peace and be made beautiful in the next life, the implication being that her disability has been eradicated through death . . . and she's better off that way.

Imagining the Future Differently

Is the elimination of disability a desired outcome for the future? Does it even occur to us to ask the question? The desire for a future without disability comes across as "common sense," but Alison Kafer in *Feminist, Queer, Crip* argues that this is only true because of "the ableist assumptions embedded in future visions." By "ableist" she means those biases that see disability as defective rather than merely a different and perfectly legitimate form of bodily existence.

It isn't disability, says Kafer, that prevents us from having a good life, but ableism, for it is ableism that leads to the pity from other people that Constance refers to. People see their lack of disability as a result of good fortune, but as Kafer mentions from her own story, while she may lead what she feels to be a satisfying life, the pity of others reminds her that they see her disability merely as something to overcome. Constance herself uses the language of overcoming disability when speaking to Addy through the medium, speaking of her admiration of Addy for all she had to overcome. It is this attitude of pity and the view that the existence and future of someone with disabilities is so bleak that leads to hardship, not necessarily the disability itself.

Discussions of disability are usually framed by one of two models: the medical model and the social model. The medical model understands disability through an individual and supposedly objective scientific view while the social model argues against the medicalization of disability and points to social structures as the cause of disability. Kafer advocates for a third option, what she calls a "political-relational model" of disability, suggesting that it is how people experience their disabilities through relationships and societal structures that make disability hard to bear.

When disability is only viewed through a supposedly unbiased medical model, issues of wheel chair accessibility are unfortunate obstacles that people with disabilities experience while waiting for a potential future cure. However, in Kafer's political-relational model, the problems that people with disabilities face are "located in inaccessible buildings, discriminatory attitudes, and ideological systems that attribute normalcy to particular minds and bodies." We cannot solve the "problem" of disability "through medical intervention or surgical normalization but through social change and political transformation."

It isn't that Kafer doesn't recognize that some people with disabilities do desire medical cures and interventions hence why she doesn't simply adopt the social model of disability. She even says, "I am not interested in becoming more disabled than I already am," but she recognizes that if our imagination for disability in the future is only limited to "curing" it, then that will affect how people with disabilities are treated and able to live in the present.

Kafer offers what she calls "a politics of crip futurity, an insistence on thinking these imagined futures . . . differently." Such a view calls into question the assumption that the only good disabled future is one in which disability is absent or cured, for if the future of disability is only imagined as cure, then there is no need to change the structures and mentality of society in the present because we are all just waiting for disability to disappear. Kafer calls this "an ethics of endless deferral." In this framework, disability is not "permitted to exist as part of a desired present or desirable future," so why change the ableist status quo and attitudes in society when disability will be eliminated in the future anyway? People with disabilities have little more to do than put their lives on hold and wait "for the cure to arrive."

But this puts people with disabilities in a more dangerous position than simply the potential of living listless and hard lives—their very survival is at stake! Not being able to imagine futures for people with disabilities has led to institutionalization, sterilization, and other forms of "violence and abuse." As we saw in *The Black Stork*, many have believed the people with disabilities are very literally better off dead, and while Constance didn't act on this impulse with Addy, one of her other children was not so lucky. As Kafer writes, "Some futures (and some bodies) are more protected than others."

The Death of Beau Langdon

Constance has a second child with a disability—Beauregard "Beau" Langdon. He suffers from a disfigurement and a mental disability. In another subversion of the eugenic logic that sees outward bodily variation as a sign of inner moral perversion, Beau is one of the most innocent and sweet ghosts in the Murder House. His presence is first hinted at in "Home Invasion" when Ben wakes up to find Addy in the basement rolling a ball back and forth with Beau, who is not seen.

We finally see Beau appear in the episode "Open House," where we also learn about his tragic backstory. The episode opens with a flashback from 1994. Constance has just received a phone call stating that Beau is going to be taken away and institutionalized, and Constance will be charged with criminal child neglect. Fearing how much Beau will suffer when he's *not* with Constance, she manipulates her boyfriend Larry Harvey, who is blindly in love with her and depicted here without the horrific burns seen in the main storyline from 2011, to "do it . . . like we discussed."

As Larry goes up to the attic, viewers discover that Constance kept Beau chained in the attic for most of his life. Larry finds Beau out of bed and wanting to play, but Larry coaxes him to bed. Waxing poetic, Larry forebodingly says, "Time to sleep. Perchance to dream. For in that sleep of death, what dreams may come?"—and then shoves a pillow into Beau's face and suffocates him to death.

In the episode "Smoldering Children," Constance, Larry, Addy, and Tate are gathered around the dinner table. As Larry is discussing taking the family to his chorus show, Addy expresses her excitement, inciting the following interaction between Tate and Constance:

> **TATE:** Don't, Addy! You're a smart girl. You know he killed our brother.
>
> **CONSTANCE:** Stop it! Beau died in his slumber of natural causes. Now you know he had a respiratory ailment. Your brother's in a better place. He suffered with every breath that he took.
>
> **TATE:** He only suffered because of you.

As with Addy's death, the result of Beau's murder is that he is now in a "better place," or in other words, as a person with a disability, he is better off dead than alive. One can also see the medical model on full display in Constance's words: "He suffered with every breath that he took." Disability, then, is an individual medical problem; however, Tate will have none of that. One can see a reflection of Kafer's political-relational model of disability when he says, "He only suffered because of you." In other words, Beau's experience of disability was made harder, not because of the disability itself, but because of how that disability was experienced through his relationship with and abuse from Constance.

In Constance's treatment of Addy and Beau, we see the inability to picture a future in which disability exists. Instead, we focus on curing or eliminating disability in the future rather than dealing with social stigmas and structural constraints upon those with disabilities in the present. Constance stigmatizes her children in the present because she cannot picture a future with their disabilities that is worth living. The message is clear—those with disabilities are better off dead than alive.

Disability and Identity

"But wait," you might say, "Is it really so wrong to want to ultimately cure disability?" You might concede that we should change social structures to accommodate those with disability and to eliminate negative social attitudes and stigmas, but in the end, a person with disabilities, while being a fully involved member of society, should be cured if such a cure is found. If a cure was found for Addy's Down syndrome, then surely she should be cured. Right? Unfortunately, this mentality reveals just how entrenched our ableist assumptions are. We need to ask a different question: If Addy and Beau were to be "cured" of their disabilities, would they still be themselves?

As Kafer points out, there are many people with disabilities who see their disability as part of what constitutes their personal identity. Kafer cites the deaf community as one example of this. While the wider culture considers the deaf disabled, many deaf people don't label themselves this way; rather, they see themselves as members of their own unique culture—complete with its own language!

Their disability has shaped them into who they are, but there is a culturally reinforced "compulsory nostalgia" or an "assumption that all disabled people long for a lost whole, pre-illness, pre-disability body." It seems, again, that the problem might not be with the disability itself; rather, it is society's structures, practices, and attitudes about disability that cause harm and suffering and keep us from imagining the presence of disability in the future as a good thing.

Making Life Livable

Whatever else can be said of Addy and Beau, their lives were made difficult by their disabilities but not in the way we are typically prone to think. So much of their suffering was due to the ableist assumptions of their mother. Her view of disability affected the lives that her children were able to lead, and in the case of Beau, one could argue that they were the direct cause of his death.

What if we could imagine disability differently? What if we could imagine futures in which people with disabilities were imagined as more than people waiting for a cure? Kafer writes, "I desire crip futures: futures that embrace disabled people, futures that imagine disability differently, futures that support multiple ways of being." Unless that happens, oppression, abuse, and death will be the lot of those with disabilities. Their existence in the present is unsafe as long as their futures, with disabilities, are unimaginable.

9
Voodoo Hoodoo

CARI CALLIS

> New Orleans Voodoo is the wild child of Voodoo's feral religions, the trick played upon the trickster.
>
> —LOUIS MARTINÉ, drummer, priest, and spiritual doctor with New Orleans Voodoo Spiritual Temple (*The Voodoo Hoodoo Spellbook*)

The third season of *American Horror Story: Coven* follows a group of Salem Witch descendants who live in a beautiful mansion in the Garden District of New Orleans called "Miss Robichaux's Academy for Exceptional Young Ladies" and it centers around their self-revelations about their individual "powers."

To make these discoveries they must first be challenged and who better to take them on than the Voodoo queen of New Orleans, Marie Laveau. This season is about Spirit Wars—the battle between the magic of Voodoo and the magic of Witchcraft. Both are spiritual practices led by women, use spells, ritual chanting, and botanical potions to heal and to either destroy or keep their enemies at bay. And both philosophies have been maligned throughout history as "dark arts" and "evil" and are often associated with Satan himself.

When Papa Legba appears as the spirit Marie Laveau has made a deal with to remain immortal, he reveals his ability to traverse the spirit world and to take individuals to their own personal version of "Hell." He conjures up the very image of Lucifer when we learn that he "owns" Laveau's soul and that she must bring him an "innocent" each year as a consideration of the deal and ultimately gives him her baby daughter. But Papa Legba is not the equivalent of Satan for those who practice Voodoo, he is rather the gatekeeper of the spirit world and a deity of communication.

To fully understand the spiritual wars between the Coven and the "Tribe" of Marie Laveau and their ultimate alliance against the Witch Hunters, we must first have some understanding of the philosophy of the practice of Voodoo and particularly the New Orleans style of Voodoo that Marie Laveaux engaged in historically.

The series acknowledges and makes use of the myth that still surrounds Marie Laveaux and her own particular brand of Voodoo service. The variances in spelling of Laveaux, which was a very common name in 1801 when Marie Laveaux was born, was used in a variety of historical documentations and is part of the reason that so much has remained a mystery about her life. The "Laveaux" spelling was the most consistent for the real Leveaux, but the character in *Coven* is credited as "Laveau". One of the most exciting and engaging aspects of the *American Horror Story*'s *Coven* is that many of the characters are based upon historical people who have been adapted as dramatic characters and whose actions in real life directly impacted the series.

My own journey to explore these historical characters began with my first experience with Voodoo when I attended a lecture and tour by Priestess Miriam in her Voodoo Spiritual Temple, focused on West African spiritual and herbal healing. It was then located on North Rampart just north of the French Quarter in New Orleans and right across the street from Congo Square where the "public" Voodoo dances were held in the nineteenth century. It has since burned down due to an electrical fire and relocated to the Marigny farther up Rampart.

Crowded into the small house with a group of sunburned tourists, I tried to focus on the lecture, which seemed to be less about the specifics of Voodoo philosophy and more about the connection of all things through vibration and energy work. In the front room there was a small store with an assortment of deities you could purchase to serve your needs; Catholic Saints, Buddha sitting next to an African Unity doll, a small section of "Priestess Miriam" brand oils and sachets for Love, Healing, and Protection.

There were several "Voudou dolls" looking nothing like the crude one stabbed repeatedly in the opening credits of *Coven*, but were instead beautiful decorative dolls dressed in traditional Senegal fabrics and with the same elaborate *tignon* or head wrap that the historical Marie Laveaux wore and that the character Marie Laveau also wears in the series. But as we were all ushered out into the small yard and stood around in a circle in the garden of that historic Creole cottage, which was unremarkable to anyone without medicinal knowledge of plants, I saw aloe, fever grass, jasmine, patchouli, rosemary, and I remembered that for Voodoo practitioners, plants have spiritual energy.

I didn't learn much about the complexity of the many forms of Voodoo philosophy that day, but I made a profound connection between plants and those who know how to recognize and use them. And I understood that Voodoo is a spiritual tradition of healing, for the body and the soul; that the core of the philosophy is about intention through prayer and using that energy to affect life in this realm. *Coven* explores the tradition of witchcraft and voodoo drawing on historical facts and blending them, as we discover, with dramatic fiction that places women in the role of leadership and magical superiority.

Voodoo and Jazz

In *The Mysterious Voodoo Queen*, Ina Johanna Fandrich insists that we can't really understand the Voodoo philosophy that the historical Marie Laveaux practiced unless we understand its African cultural and religious origins. It still exists in three distinct places: Benin in West Africa, Haiti in the Caribbean, and Southern Louisiana in the United States.

She clarifies the different spellings, *Vodun* is the traditional indigenous religion of Benin and as such one of the oldest religious traditions on this planet; *Vodou* is a highly developed mystical religion that emerged under the trauma of slavery as an assertion of resistance on the island of Haiti; and *Voodoo* is a similar but different African-based religion that enslaved Africans and free people of color (*gens de couleur libre*) created simultaneously in colonial Louisiana.

As Fandrich discovered through meticulous research into Laveaux's history, it's difficult to understand her practice of New Orleans Voodoo if you only draw from Eurocentric sources—newspapers, police reports, census, court and property records, notary entries, and travel accounts of the time. The first eyewitness reports of the persecuted religious practice were not recorded until around 1930 and they were the elderly recalling events from their childhood. Fandrich compares New Orleans Voodoo to the music of Jazz, both born in the same place—Congo Square in New Orleans—and both incorporating elements of European, Haitian, and Native American traditions and influences with their foundation being fundamentally African. Some historians have even said that without Laveaux and her popular "Voodoo dances" jazz might never have been born.

Jazz plays an important role in the entire season of *Coven*, not surprising for a story set in New Orleans. Fiona, the Supreme, falls for Axeman, the sax player whose haunting tunes remind us of both the history of the birth of jazz and the modern evolution of it. The season's soundtrack includes everyone from Coleman Hawkins, Louis Armstrong, and Papa Mali to the Preservation Hall Jazz Band. It features jazz prominently when Marie Laveau is onscreen.

In 1724 the French established Code Noire or The Black Code laws for both the slaves and their masters to live by. Slaves were given Sunday afternoons off to meet and to trade goods, play music and dance and sell things in order to potentially buy their way to freedom. Congo Square in New Orleans was the gathering place for both the slaves and the free people of color to socialize and the only place drums were allowed. These very same drummers who pounded out the beat for the Bamboula dancers in the afternoon were the ones that provided the drumming for the Voodoo dances that were held in secret places at night because the public gathering of slaves and free people of color was forbidden other than on Sunday afternoons. No religious practice, except for Roman Catholicism, was allowed.

Jazz and Voodoo are intimately connected and the sexual aspect of that connection is never more clear than when the Axeman, also based upon a real person, a serial killer active in New Orleans in 1918–19 seduces Fiona as he makes references to his instrument ("The Dead"). The Axeman tells us he has a "close relationship with the Angel of Death" and that he's not human, but a spirit and a "felled demon from the hottest hell." His crime against humanity is his role as a serial killer who is himself killed when he is challenged by a young witch, Millie, who plays an Aria instead of the jazz the Axeman has insisted must be played throughout New Orleans or else he will kill those who don't comply. This is exactly what the historical Axeman, who was never caught, required of the citizens in New Orleans. And as in the series the jazz musicians and the dance halls were jammed.

By the time Laveaux was born, the French were being overthrown in St. Domingue, now known as Haiti, by a successful slave rebellion fueled by the practice of Voodoo ritual. The New Orleans community of plantation slave owners weren't taking any chances that their slaves and the free people of color plot another rebellion like the one that had been so successful in Haiti, so the Voodoo rituals were held in the swampy St. John's Bayou, warehouses, businesses, and secluded back yards. The influx of Haitian refugees only added to the strength of Voodoo's effectiveness in uniting the black community. The Voodoo drums went underground to survive. This driving beat which invites the spirits and the improvisational nature of jazz, like New Orleans Voodoo, is what Fandrich calls, "a synthesis of an African and an American identity."

I Put a Spell on You

In the first episode of *American Horror Story*: *Coven*, Marie Laveau arrives at Madame LaLaurie's mansion to exact revenge for the brutal mutilation of her lover Bastien, by delivering a love potion that promises to cure LaLaurie's husband's compulsion for young ladies and to ensure fidelity, but instead, knocks her out, kills her entire family and renders her immortal. She is buried alive for eternity—never to be reunited in the afterlife with her loved ones—as punishment for her treatment of all slaves, until Fiona digs her up two centuries later. Fiona wants the one thing that her enemy possesses, the ability to be immortal and to make another person immortal, but she doesn't know the price that Laveau has paid ("Bitchcraft").

Then Fiona goes to the Ninth Ward hair salon, Cornrow City, to bargain with Laveau to give her the Voodoo secret by hinting that she has something that Laveau wants ("Boy Parts"). The historical Laveaux was also a hairdresser and most likely she didn't have a salon but traveled to client's homes to do their hair. Imagine all of the inside info she could get from the live-in servants and slaves that could reveal their masters' darkest secrets. Everyone knows you tell your hairdresser everything. In this first confrontation between Fiona and Laveau, the fictional history of Laveau's Voodoo Tribe and the Witches' Salem lineage is revealed to have originated from the Arawak shamans who gave the Voodoo Tribe the "secrets of the other side—Necromancy."

Laveau tells Fiona: "Everything you got, you got from us." Fiona doesn't exactly deny the history but dismisses the idea that "Tituba, a Voodoo slave girl who wouldn't know a love potion from a chocolate chip cookie recipe if she had to *read* it," gave them their power. But Laveau reminds her that it was Tituba who gave the gift of witchcraft to the Witches and the Salem Witches betrayed her.

The historical Tituba was the first person to be accused of witchcraft during the 1692 Salem Witch trials and there are theories that she may have told the other girls accused and those that she named as her accomplices, about her knowledge of Voodoo. She later confessed she learned techniques from her mistress in Barbados about how to protect herself from evil. Over the years through the fictional representations of her, she morphed into African American, African, half Indian and half Black but she was actually listed as "Indian Woman, servant" in the trial documents, and other historical documents point to her coming from an Arawak Village, where she was sold into slavery and then sent to Barbados where Voodoo was practiced. She was then bought by her accuser, Reverend Samuel Parrish, and taken to Salem, Massachusetts.

Coven's writers adapted this historical event to create the centuries-old rivalry between the Witches and the Voodoo Tribe. Whether the historical Tituba practiced Voodoo or not, this story demonstrates that from the earliest mention of witchcraft, it was connected to Voodoo and maligned as punishable by death if practiced. Poor Tituba confessed and made up a wild story that sounded nothing like anything connected to Voodoo, but she survived, which is more than can be said for the rest of the Salem witch trial victims.

These scenes with Laveau quickly introduce us to two different but essential aspects of the belief system of Voodoo. The first is the use of that love potion, which LaLaurie says tastes like honeysuckle as she drinks it. The role of a Voodoo priestess in her community is to use the natural elements, plants, roots, herbs, and other botanicals to effect change in the physical realm whether it's to cure yellow fever or keep a lover from straying. By all accounts the historical Laveaux worked tirelessly as a nurse during the yellow fever and cholera epidemics allegedly saving many lives. She worked side by side with one of her closest friends, Father Antonio de Sedella, or Père Antoine as he was known, the beloved Spanish priest of St. Louis Cathedral of which Laveaux and her family were life-long members and where they attended mass daily with other women of color who owned their own businesses, walked the streets proudly, and took great pride in their appearance.

Marie's birth and death records, baptism, marriage and birth of her children, are all known only because of her membership in the Catholic Church. Laveaux's practice of Voodoo didn't interfere with her Catholic beliefs and she incorporated the use of the saints and specific prayers to invoke their aid as a part of her practice.

New Orleans Voodoo survived because it adapted the Voodoo spirits, the "loa" sometimes spelled lwa, with Catholic names that embodied the characteristics associated with the personality of the Saint. But the Virgin Mary, St. Peter, the Saints, and the angels are not the same as the loa, although they serve a similar purpose and that's to directly connect to one God, the creator, called Bon Dieu or Good God. But as Denise Alvarado, a Creole Voodoo practitioner explains, "The Voodooists' relationship with the loa differs from saints and angels in that the loa are not merely petitioned with prayer—they are served" (*Voodoo Hoodoo Spellbook*, p. 25).

The second important aspect is associating Voodoo with necromancy—the communication with the dead and the ability to call up and communicate with ancestral spirits as well as the loa, to affect the living. The Haitians who practice Voudou would not find this unnatural or an unusual occurrence in their daily lives. Maya Deren, the artist and filmmaker who first documented the Haitian deities, practitioners, and rituals of Voudou through her field work and personal experiences, went to Haiti to make a movie about ritual dances and ended up becoming a Voudou initiate.

When she completed her film *Divine Horsemen: The Living Gods of Haiti* she then, at the urging of Joseph Campbell, wrote her reflections on her experiences in her book with the same title. Voudou, she writes,

> proposes that man has a material body, animated by an *esprit* or *gros-bon-ange*—the soul, spirit, psyche or self—which being non-material, does not share the death of the body. This soul may achieve the status of a *loa*, a divinity, and become the archetypal representative of some natural or moral principle. As such, it has the power to displace temporarily the *gros-bon-ange* of a living per-

son and become the animating force of his physical body. (*Divine Horsemen*, p. 15)

This psychic phenomenon is known as "possession." Deren's firsthand experiences reveal what it might be like to be possessed as Campbell summarized it in the foreword he wrote for her book:

> Maya Deren spoke of her own experiences of possession, telling of the power of the drums as they drove the god (the loa, the mystère) into the body of the devotee (the serviteur); also, as she described the pranks and characteristics of the various mystères when they had mounted (monté) i.e., taken possession of, a worshipper. Every loa had his own drum beat, his own manner of behavior, his own costume (which was immediately installed on the monté as soon as the loa present was identified), and his own domain of spiritual revelation—through all of which, as Maya talked, I could readily recognize the motifs already familiar to me from the myths of the high religions, not only of antiquity, but also of the modern East and West.

Both aspects of the Voodooists' role in the community are synthesized when Cordelia goes to Laveau to ask her to perform the Voodoo fertility ritual called *Pochaut Medecine* involving some sperm, a goat, and a guinea pepper ("The Replacements"). As Laveau narrates what happens in the ritual if she agrees to perform it, Cordelia sees herself participate in it and this is the first Voodoo ceremony that reveals how Laveau's magic works.

The drums invoke the dance and Laveau eats the guinea pepper to get the spirit's attention by her sacrifice and willingness to suffer. The goat is sacrificed over the participant and Laveau becomes possessed by the spirit who gives her the power to effect this change. Animal sacrifice is not used in all Voodoo communities, but the first-hand accounts of the historical Laveaux say that sacrificing a chicken was common at the Voodoo dances and that it was then tossed into a large pot and used to feed the community after the ceremony.

Offerings to the spirits in the form of food is common in many religions and each specific loa has a preference for certain things including rum and tobacco.

Zombie versus Li Grand Zombi

Laveau has the knowledge to create Zombies. She calls them up from the grave to kill the white supremacists who lynch her client's son. The ritual required to raise the dead and send them on a killing spree involves a lot more than a guinea pepper and a goat ("Fearful Pranks Ensue").

Zombies are an aspect of New Orleans Voodoo that has its roots in Haitian Vodou. A zombie is a living person who has been given a drug and buried alive and is later dug up by a *bokor*, or a *bocor* as Deren describes them, "the professional magician, who deals with zombies and in *baka* (malevolent spirits contained in the form of various animals)" (*Divine Horsemen*, p. 75). Is this what Bastien has become: a baka spiritual slave of Laveau? This type of priest is not working to heal but is making a financial deal with a dark spirit and practicing ritual magic. Actual documented reports of zombies are few and far between, but they too are a part of the myth of the historical Laveaux.

There's no evidence that Laveaux was a bokor, and she maintained a reputation as a healer especially during the yellow fever epidemics. But just as Laveau uses her zombies as a way to get justice for the lynching of the young boy, the historical Laveaux is believed by New Orleanian community historian Randall Mitchell to have given this zombie powder to death row inmates and then had them dug up after the poison wore off and sent on their way to freedom.

In defense of Mitchell's theory, Fandrich weighs out the evidence and considers it plausible. Laveaux did live across the square from the prison, boats went back and forth daily to Haiti, and zombie powder was in use enough to be outlawed in 1846. There is an 1871 newspaper article that documents the elderly Marie Laveaux preparing an all-white altar for two condemned prisoners (pp. 167–68).

Marie Laveau doesn't perform the ritual to raise the zombies for personal gain, but to avenge a perceived wrong, just as the mythical stories about the historical Laveaux reveal that she was motivated by moral considerations. There are stories about her purchasing slaves and setting them free, and allegedly might even have been a part of the underground railroad. She was said to have influenced court cases in order to save young men from the gallows and young women from imposed marriages.

One of the most unique aspects of New Orleans Voodoo that differentiates it from West African and Haitian Voudou is its intimate connections with the Catholic Church through prayer and the connections to the Virgin Mary and many saints and angels. Pope John Paul II attended a Voodoo ceremony in 1993 and spoke out in support of recognizing the spiritual roots of African tradition. In New Orleans, the two coexist as they have done since the slaves first set foot in the city.

Practitioners managed to keep their connection to their ancestors, their direct connection to the spirits that protected and healed them, and their commitment to the divine force of *one* god. Voodoo evolved into something different when it was practiced by generations who had never been to Africa. It doesn't have a sacred text or a prescribed doctrine and so it is an oral tradition incorporating the wisdom of what the slaves gathered from what they observed and saw around them.

The Catholic aspect of New Orleans Voodoo is not referenced when Marie Laveau performs the ritual to send the Zombies to kill the rednecks in the shed. However, the ceremony does reference the most important deity in Voodoo and that's the Sky Father Damballa Wedo, who is also called Li Grande Zombi, the serpent spirit who created the universe. Laveau calls the spirit by drawing its *vévé* in chalk The *vévé* is a sacred symbol that acts like a sort of batman signal to call the particular spirit she wants to work with. She makes the offering by killing the snake and providing a handful of pearls for extra measure. The drums help to induce her trance and she is mounted by the spirit which gives her the power to raise the zombies.

There are firsthand accounts and songs about the historical Laveaux dancing both with a serpent named Li Grande Zombi and imitating the movements of a snake. Witnesses claim she was able to undulate her body exactly as a serpent and nearly every account vividly recalls the powerful effect that her dancing had upon the audience and the participants. Li Grande Zombi comes from the Kikongo word *nzambi* meaning "the almighty God" and it is generally accepted that Laveaux contributed to the religious movement that is still popular and practiced today.

The Epic Battle

The second time Laveau calls up the zombies is to get revenge against Fiona who dug up Madame LaLaurie and killed Bastien. The ritual is successful, the zombies attack, but they are stopped by a power stronger than Laveau's, the young witch Zoe. As Laveau controls them by levitating above the vévé, she comes crashing down when Zoe sets her intention and breaks the spell. And then it's revealed that Hank, Cordelia's husband, is a witch killer hired by Laveau to kill them all. He could not go through with it—he double-crossed Laveau and killed the entire Voodoo Tribe. Laveau only managed to escape because Queenie sacrificed herself. Laveau is humbled and goes to the witches and meets with Fiona to unite together to kill the Witch Hunters.

This is a provocative twist because the gender roles are so clearly defined. The female Supreme and the Voodoo Queen are united against the all-male witch killers. New Orleans Voodoo has always been dominated by powerful women and it was racially inclusive from the beginning. Several white women were included in the arrest reports of those who were caught and jailed. The spiritual tradition of Voodoo can be led by a male or a female and, according to tradition, the spirits are not particular when it comes to the gender of who they possess. In Voodoo, a woman literally becomes the deity, and it's pretty clear that Laveau does exactly that when she becomes possessed and calls up the zombies to attack the witches. The vévé used in her ritual is drawn with a heart so Laveau may be possessed by Erzulie Dantor. Her tignon, the elaborate head wrap that slaves and women of color were by law forced to wear and which they turned into a crown of glory, is red, so surely she's calling upon one of the Petro loa, which are the fiery, more aggressive spirits which originated in Haiti during the battle for their freedom. She's the most powerful of these fierce spirits and is associated with revenge and aggression.

But ultimately the epic battle is not between the powerful women, because Laveau's followers are massacred by Hank, the son of head Director of the all-male witch hunters, known as The Corporation, who are defeated by Fiona and Laveau first by their wits when they take down the company and then hacked to pieces ("Protect the Coven"). This battle is not unlike the one for the survival of Voodoo and witchcraft, threatened and persecuted but managing to survive and adapt all the same.

Immortality and Papa Legba

The most powerful characters of the series, Fiona and Laveau, have the same obsession with immortality. Laveau has achieved it and Fiona wants it above all else. Papa Legba, the guardian of the crossroads between worlds, is the most important character in the Voodoo pantheon because he's the one that offers admittance to the spirit world for both the living and the dead, not unlike his Catholic counterpart St. Peter. As Deren describes him (p. 97), he's the link between the visible mortal world and the invisible, immortal world. All communication with the loa goes through him and he is the first and last person invoked in a ceremony. He's not a demon or Satan, not good nor evil, but a trickster.

And just like Erzulie, he has a Rada or cooler side, and a hotter Petro side where he's known as Kalfu. He doesn't fit the description of the kind old man of Papa Legba who wears a straw hat, smokes a pipe, and sprinkles water, but appears in black with glowing red eyes and a top hat. He's a man of words, a cunning communicator known to speak all languages. But how does his ability to confine souls to Hell as he does in *Coven* resonate with the spiritual beliefs of Voodoo?

Voodooists believe in a kind of heaven, and that Hell is here on Earth in a bodiless spirit. After death the *gros bon ange*, the body, and the *ti bon ange*, the spirit must be sent to where they belong or the dead person's spirit can become trapped. They can be controlled psychically. This is the true zombie.

Marie Laveau doesn't achieve true immortality and she is separated from her body when she is chopped into many pieces and buried separately. Queenie reminds Papa Legba that she can no longer complete her part of the bargain and so she is trapped in her own private hell with Madame LaLaurie and is forced to torture her. Laveau pleads with Papa Legba when she learns she is dead because she can no longer fulfill her part of the bargain, "But I was good to people, I protected so many." Legba reminds her of the innocents she brought him for centuries, and that "Everybody pays. Everybody suffers." Papa Legba here sums up the premise of the series, and the core belief of most religions including Voodoo ("Go to Hell").

Even Fiona is trapped in a hell of her own making as the Axeman tells her when she finds that after death she's stuck with him in a cabin reeking of fish and knotty pine ("The Seven Wonders"). She too has lost her soul, her *gros bon ange* and her *ti bon ange* have been separated indefinitely. Fiona and Marie Laveau have become ghosts and from the Voodoo perspective there is nothing greater to be feared.

And what of the real Marie Laveaux, did she find immortality? In a way she did. She became a loa in the pantheon of New Orleans Voodoo deities. She lived in a time and place where women of color had little or no power in any area of their lives and she was known for her strength and influence but she was always an enigma even when she was alive.

On the day of her death in 1881 two eulogies were posted that sum up her complexity. *The Daily Picayune* praised her with the headline, "A Woman with a Wonderful History, almost a Century Old—Carried to the Tomb Yesterday Evening." The reporter goes on to talk about her upstanding family, her renowned beauty, her charitable work for the sick and condemned prisoners, and her close relationships with everyone from the Governor to Aaron Burr and Lafayette.

He sums up her life with: "All in all Marie Laveau was a most wonderful woman. Doing good for the sake of doing good alone . . ." There is not a single mention of Voodoo in the summary of her life and work. The emphasis is on her Catholic service and devotion. The next day the *New Orleans Democrat* ran their own headline, "A Sainted Woman," which begins by asking "Who has been stuffing our contemporaries in the matter of the defunct Voudou queen, Marie Lavoux?" The reporter goes on to say, "The fact is, the least said about Marie Lavoux's sainted life, etc., the better. She was, up to an advanced age, the prime mover and soul of the indecent orgies of the ignoble Voudous: and to her influence may be attributed the fall of many a virtuous woman." And he ends with, "But talk about her morality and kiss her sainted brow—puah!!" (*Mysterious Voodoo Queen*, pp. 172–75).

The Gates of Guinee

We can never completely know what kind of rituals and belief system the historical Laveaux actually practiced in her role as Voodoo Queen. We're left to look most closely at the practice that emerged and grew from her legacy, and from the streets she walked so proudly and fearlessly in the French Quarter, where she is still alive for tourists, scholars and spiritual seekers. Her religion, her ancestors, and her myth live on, and the character of Laveau in *Coven* embodies all of the complexities that the real Laveaux must have also had. She is deliciously dramatized as a character possessing both moral integrity and capable of savage acts of brutality.

Voodooists believe that the dead must cross the Gate of Guinee, and obtain permission from Baron Samedi to enter where all of the loa reside. Deren describes it as "Africa, the

10
Too Freaking Bad

ROD CARVETH

The fourth season of *American Horror Story* is set in a freak show in the early 1950s. A freak show is a performance showcase of a variety of *stigmatized* individuals, commonly known as "freaks."

P.T. Barnum had a long-running "freak show" at his American Museum in New York City. Barnum featured individuals with physical stigmas such as the miniature Tom Thumb, a black mother with two albino children, a bearded lady, the giantess Anna Swan and the Tattooed Man (George Contentenus, who had 338 tattoos covering his body). In the United States, the freak show had its peak years between the 1840s and 1940s. Thus, as *American Horror Story: Freak Show* opens, the popularity of the freak show is beginning an inexorable decline among forms of American entertainment.

While there are several storylines that permeate the season's episodes, the principal theme that Ryan Murphy communicates is that the freaks are individuals being judged unfairly, being ridiculed or persecuted simply because they're different, and subsequently forced to inhabit the fringes of society. Elsa, the proprietor of the show, rails against the people in the community, charging that they are the actual monsters.

Ironically, while Murphy explores the exploitation of the freaks during the season, the series itself is exploitative. The theme song for the series is, "Come look at the freaks, Come gape at the geeks, Come examine these aberrations, Their malformations, Grotesque physiques, Only pennies for peeks." Thus, the series is telling the TV audience the focus is on these "abominations of the body." Further, able-bodied actors and actresses, whose deformities are not real, work on the series with people who have real life deformities, such as dwarfism, flipper arms, and missing legs. As a result, there is actually a real-life freak show within a fictional freak show.

In telling a story about the exploitation of freaks—many of whom have "blemishes of individual character," such as being serial killers—actual "freaks" are being exploited. In addition, by featuring many of the characters as evil or insane, does the series enlarge the gap between virtual social identity and actual social identity for the actors with real physical deformities in the series—an act that may be the real horror story of this chapter of *American Horror Story*?

The Appeal of the Freak Show

The term "stigma" originates from the Greek term for "bodily sign"—or a mark that indicated a person was tainted somehow. In his 1963 book *Stigma*, sociologist Erving Goffman provided an in-depth analysis of the meanings of stigma. Goffman described stigma as a personal attribute, behavior, or reputation that is socially discrediting to the point that it will cause the person viewing the individual with a stigma to view that person as an undesirable: "He is thus reduced in our minds from a whole and usual person to a tainted, discounted one."

Goffman further argues that the character traits we assign to the stigmatized individual are that person's virtual social identity. By contrast, the attributes that a stigmatized individual really possesses constitute the person's actual social identity. The degree to which a person with a stigma will be viewed negatively will be the degree to which there is a gap between the virtual social identity and the actual social identity.

Goffman defines three categories of stigma: "abominations of the body" (such as physical disabilities); "blemishes of individual character" (such as "moral" failings like pathological liars); and "tribal stigma" (such as race, religion, or ethnicity). Goffman also proposes that certain stigmas are viewed so negatively that they will always be abnormal and deviant (such as being a child molester). While most "blemishes of individual character" and "tribal stigmas" (except for race) are often invisible, most "abominations of the body" are visible. Thus, individuals with stigmas of this type are most easily identified. People viewing individuals with such stigma are repulsed by the deformities, but, at the same time, relieved that they do not have them.

Goffman proposed that stigmatized persons are devalued, even ostracized. As a result, individuals who are perceived to have some stigmatized condition have fewer opportunities to succeed in life. Those opportunities are limited, said Goffman, because others believe that the stigmatized individual lacks moral character or is not normal. Thus, argued Goffman, stigma "spoils" the social identity of the person possessing one, preventing the stigmatized person from having deserved social acceptance, and, often self-acceptance.

The characteristic a stigmatized individual possesses is not necessarily evil, but is perceived as deviant because of the culture's values. As such, those characteristics that are deemed "stigma" are not culturally universal and may evolve over time. For example, the desirable rounded curves of the women Peter Paul Rubens painted in the seventeenth century were perceived negatively in the 1990s when a standard of a desirable female physique was model Kate Moss. Still, a person labeled as possessing a stigma is subject to powerful social and psychological forces that not only determine how a culture perceives stigmatized individuals, but how stigmatized individuals perceive themselves.

In addition to the stigmas of body, character, and social demography, Goffman distinguishes between stigma that is "discredited" (an individual's stigma that is evident or known) versus stigma that is "discreditable" (an individual's stigma that is not immediately apparent). For those whose stigma is discredited—such as a physical deformity or traumatic injury such as a major facial scar—there are few options that an individual has to manage his or her "spoiled identity." Those individuals whose stigma is discreditable (such as those that have a mental illness or are HIV-positive) have more options in terms of managing the information about the stigma. Managing the information about the stigma, however, can cause stress and anxiety about what, when, and to whom to disclose the stigma. For example, some homeless people are discredited—they are seen living on the streets or in train stations. They can't hide the stigma of being homeless. Other homeless people live in their cars, and thus can better manage the stigma of being homeless.

There are a number of behaviors that individuals with stigmas engage in. Stigmatized individuals might avoid situations in which they feel uncomfortable (even to the point of becoming socially isolated). They might make efforts to conceal the stigma, such as trying to pass themselves off as normal. Stigmatized individuals may avoid hanging out with people of the same condition in order to avoid being reminded of their own stigma. All of these behaviors serve to reinforce the fact that the individuals are living with a condition others perceive to not be normal.

Of course, the perceptions that a stigma will lead to discrimination by others is not just in the heads of the people with stigma. In terms of stigma, there are two groups—one that is characterized as normal and one group that is characterized as stigmatized. The normal group has those attributes seen as necessary and desirable by society, while the stigmatized group possesses attributes which are seen as negative and discrediting by society. As Goffman states:

> By definition, of course, we believe the person with a stigma is not quite human. On this assumption, we exercise varieties of discrimination, through which we effectively, often unthinkingly, reduce his life chances.

Goffman's basic thesis states that the extent to which a person is stigmatized and plays that role is based on how obvious a stigma is, its negative value in society, and how well the stigma is managed. Furthermore, the obvious aspect of the stigma and its negative value can be manipulated by how well a person manages the negative attribute(s), through the process of impression.

A stigma operates as a master status, a status that has special importance for one's social identity, often shaping a person's entire life. As such, not only does the master status impact the individual's perception of herself, but "normals" dehumanize those with stigmas by viewing them only in terms of their stigma (such as the person in the wheelchair, or the person with the scar). It is not surprising, then, that entrepreneurs would capitalize on the discomfort, relief, and curiosity of the "normal" people about such physical "freaks."

Freak Shows

Bodies that are visually problematic (scars, missing limbs, deformities) have always been more conspicuous than the bodies of those who are not visually problematic or so-called "normal." Freak shows transformed everyday encounters between "deviants" and "normal" into entertainment. The dramatization of the encounter between "freak" and "normal" American citizens provided freak performers an opportunity to be able to freely display their visible stigmas in ways that would be prohibited in everyday life.

Though the exhibition of "different" bodies has a long history, the freak show emerged as a popular form of American entertainment in the mid-nineteenth century. The freak show encompassed traveling companies in the United States and Europe, and dime museums as well as exhibitions at carnivals, fairs, and circuses.

Most credit P.T. Barnum with the beginning of the freak show in the United States. He began his show business career with the presentation of Joice Heth, an African American woman billed as being 161 years old and a nurse present at the birth of George Washington. Allegedly, when Barnum acquired Heth in 1835, among her official papers was a bill of sale dated 1727 that listed her age as fifty-four years old. Barnum promoted Heth as "a remarkable curiosity" and he credited her exhibition as the official start of his career as a showman. Though his acts were subjected to uncomfortable, often judgmental, scrutiny, Barnum treated and paid his acts well.

The rise in popularity of freak shows directly corresponded to the social and cultural changes occurring in a nineteenth-century America marked by the Industrial Revolution, while the growth of industrial technology led to the United States becoming a more economically competitive global power. On the other hand, these changes not only transformed the family and gender roles, as well as drawing millions of immigrants looking for economic opportunity, it also led to a virtual plague of disabilities from work-related injuries—thus creating people stigmatized by their "abominations of the body."

In earlier eras, babies born with serious deformities were referred to as "monsters." Their appearance was regarded as an evil omen, a sign of divine retribution, and a prediction of disasters to come (the word "monster," in fact, is derived from the Latin verb, *monere*, which means to warn or foretell). Oftentimes deformed children were killed or abandoned and left to die. Aristotle opposed the feeding of deformed and disabled children, while Plato proposed that infirm and deformed children be hidden from view. Christianity in the Middle Ages argued that if people were made in God's image, "monsters" must be the work of the devil. While in early modern Western culture freaks were often regarded as symbolic of moral and religious weakness, by the mid-nineteenth century the new professions of science and medicine proposed that "freaks" were primarily deviant human types and, as a result, scientists and doctors used freaks as test subjects to propose new theories of the human body.

Finally, the expansion of the United States as a global player brought Americans into direct contact with non-Western ("exotic") peoples more than ever before. Freak shows often featured "exotic" individuals. These exotic individuals, however, were portrayed as primitive and savage, and thus inferior to their American audience. This served to reassure customers that, despite all the changes in society, their superior status in the world remained unchanged.

Freak show historian Robert Bogdan identified five primary types of freaks who were typically displayed in the nineteenth-century freak show:

1. **natural or born freaks (individuals born with physical or mental disabilities);**
2. **non-Western freaks or "exotic ethnics" (individuals who were generally non-disabled but who were classified as freakish due to their ascribed ethnic or racial identity);**
3. **self-made freaks (individuals who modified their bodies in order to achieve freak status);**
4. **novelty artists (individuals considered freakish through their engagement in unconventional types of performance such as sword-swallowing, fire-eating, or snake-charming); and**
5. **gaffed or "fake" freaks (individuals who manufactured a physical disability, for example through the use of a prosthetic limb).**

Bogdan also noted that freaks were generally presented in one of two ways. The first way was in an aggrandized mode of presentation where the freak was conferred a grandiose and dignified status, such as P.T. Barnum's presentation of "General" Tom Thumb. In addition, an aggrandized freak often possessed special abilities, such as a high intelligence. As such, an aggrandized freak could be seen to have a superior status to the average freak-show attendee, yet that status was tempered because of the nature of being a freak. Many aggrandized freaks, such as Joseph Merrick ("The Elephant Man") became celebrities.

The other mode is known as exotic mode, which was an attribution made because of the freak's ethnic or racial status. Exotic freaks, such as the "Wild Man of Borneo," were often shown in exotic settings (such as a "jungle"), complete with tribal garb and an extensive backstory. Some exotic freaks came from non-Western areas of the world, but others were ethnic-looking Americans made up to appear exotic.

Freak shows also raised the possibility of transgressive sex and of challenging norms of gender and sexuality. The unconventional bodies of freaks allowed audiences to contemplate ambiguous sex (in the case of hermaphrodites), group sex (in the case of conjoined twins—such as with Dot and Bette in "Freak Show"), grotesque sex (in the case of those exhibited as "fat" boys and girls), interracial sex (in the case of "exotic ethnics"), and titillating sex (consider the case of "Freak Show," with Jimmy pleasuring women at a Tupperware party with his deformed hands), in addition to questioning traditional boundaries between male and female bodies. Thus, the portrayals of sex and sexuality raised by freak shows allowed audiences to consider changing norms of gender and sexuality within an acceptable form of entertainment.

Freak Shows Decline

The decline of the freak show in American culture came about largely because of two major changes in society.

The first change came about in terms of the social attitude toward "freaks." In part led by the medical profession who saw many of the individuals with visible stigmas as suffering from diseases or other pathological conditions that should be treated and corrected to make them appear more "normal," freaks were increasingly seen as individuals who should be hidden from public view—not in the home, but, rather, in institutions where they could be "taken care of" (code for a socially acceptable banishment). As a result, the notion of putting people with obvious stigmas on stage for entertainment and profit was considered inappropriate.

The second change came about due to technological developments in forms of popular entertainment, particularly television. Television could create more and more wild and bizarre monsters and bring them into people's living rooms. The real-life monsters of the freak show were outshined by their on-screen counterparts. Ironically, over time, the fictional monsters of scripted television had to compete with the types of "oddities" that used to be featured in freak shows, with "reality TV" shows devoted to dwarves and 600-pound people.

Exploiting Stigmas

One of the characteristics of the first four seasons of *American Horror Story* is that there is a focus on societal "deviants" who have banded together as a family. In the televised storyline of *Freak Show*, this family is made up of a group who stand out because of their genetic deformities. This family is further solidified by the fact that they are part of a freak show—and thus are making money from the very reactions of "normals" who are paying to see "deviants," the same deviants who in an everyday setting would be receiving their disdain for free.

When the nurse, Millie, whom Elsa drugged and brought back to the show's camp in order to get Dot and Bette, charged that the show's characters were "depraved," Elsa shot back:

> I'll tell you who the monsters are. The people outside this tent. In your town, in all these little towns. Housewives pinched with bitterness, stupefied with boredom as they doze off in front of their laundry detergent commercials and dream of strange erotic monsters. My monsters, the ones you called depraved, they are the beautiful, heroic ones. They offer their odyssey to the world. They provide a laugh or fright to people in need of entertainment. ("Monsters Among Us")

Elsa makes two important points here. The first is that the "freaks" are her family. Not only are they not depraved, it is society who is depraved in the way that they treat "the monsters." The "bad guys" are the society that has created the conditions where these folks can't live normal lives because of their visible differences, or the Motts, who view the freaks as exotic pets to be purchased.

Elsa's second point is that what the freaks are doing is their choice—they are *offering* "their odyssey to the world." In the second half of the twentieth century, states such as California and Florida tried to ban freak shows, but the courts ruled that doing so was unconstitutional. The courts ruled that to argue that "freaks" are being exploited shows a lack of respect to the freaks—that despite the fact that many of these human "oddities" are adults, they are seen as incapable of being able to consent to being a part of the show. In other words, if those people with visible stigma are supposed to have the same rights and mental abilities as everyone else, then they should be able to negotiate financial agreements for performing.

Ironically, what Ryan Murphy has put together here in terms of his cast combines actual differently-abled performers playing secondary characters compared to the stars who are using prosthetics. Jyoti Amge, the world's smallest woman, plays Ma Petite, whose performance in the freak show consists of standing in a small cage onstage. Trans-actress Erika Ervin (a.k.a. Amazon Eve) plays the world's strongest woman. Mat Fraser portrays Paul the Illustrated Seal, a man with "flipper" arms (Fraser, who has been a successful drummer, was born with phocomelia). Finally, there's Legless Suzi, played by Rosie Siggins, who was born with sacral agenesis, which led to the amputation of her deformed legs. These real-life individuals who have visible stigma are making good money being part of "Freak Show." Their appearance in the show should also help with generating other income-producing opportunities.

The roles provided by Murphy were rare opportunities for these individuals to work in front of the camera. Fraser, fifty-five, did have ten other acting credits before *Freak Show* according to the Internet Movie Database. Erika Ervin had four credits, while Rose Siggins and Jyoti Amge had none (Siggins and Amge had appeared on TV and film as themselves). So, if options for acting are limited—and even then, limited to playing freaks—how much freedom did they truly have to consent given that they lacked any meaningful choice?

None of these actors were the stars of *American Horror Story: Freak Show*. The stars were able-bodied actors who through a combination of prosthetics and special camera effects become "freaks." These actors included Evan Peters as Jimmy Darling, lobster boy; the carnival's bearded lady played by Kathy Bates; Sarah Paulson's conjoined twins, Dot and Bette; Angela Bassett as a three-breasted woman or Jessica Lange's legless Elsa Mars. As a result, the real life differently abled "freaks" are the series's window dressing.

The issue runs deeper than this, however. Essentially, exploitation is a form of power where the exploiter benefits from some characteristic of the exploited and does so at the exploited's expense. On the one hand, the freak show operator (exploiter) benefits from the freak's labor in terms of ticket sales. But, the freaks (exploited) also benefit from the material benefits provided by the freak show owners.

But not all exploitation is material. There are non-material aspects of exploitation, such as the loss of a person's *dignity*. If dignity is conceived of as the equal value of people, then benefitting from other people by putting them in an unequal position would undermine their dignity. So, while the freak show operator may provide material benefits to the freaks, the operator does so at the expense of the non-material consideration of their dignity.

There is also an issue of consent. Most freaks have few alternatives to work for a living, given the scorn that they receive in the outside world. If alternatives are so restricted, the question arises as to whether the freaks' consent to work is true consent, or is the result of only picking from the severely restricted choices available. Thus, in portraying a group of individuals who suffer non-material losses to their dignity while obtaining the material benefits of support from a freak show operator, Murphy is actually doing the same thing to the "freaks" he is employing in his series.

Hurt or Helped?

On one level, *American Horror Story: Freak Show* is a story about how badly society treats some of its most vulnerable members. On another level, the story is about the empowerment of those same individuals, though that empowerment manifests itself in often criminal ways, such as the murder by Jimmy of the detective investigating the murder of the mother of Dot and Bette, and the subsequent "elimination" of the body by the performers.

Freak Show is also about unintended consequences. When Elsa sold the freak show to Dandy Mott, she could not have envisioned that nearly all of the performers would be murdered by Mott.

In employing "freaks" as freaks, Ryan Murphy likely thought that he was doing a socially responsible act. But, like many aspects of actual freak shows, that interpretation is not so clear-cut.

III

I have long stopped asking why the mad do mad things

11
999 Fingers

CHRISTOPHER KETCHAM

The fingers thing? Later. Be patient.

You asked who I am. Who created me? What am I doing here? Why do I look like this? Or at least that's what you're thinking. All in good time.

My creator first. Always must start with a creator because there is nothing that can be before the creator, right? Maybe for you and your Abrahamic God, but what about others who don't have one? What if you are a Buddhist and there is no God to have created anything? Say you are Friedrich Nietzsche who just killed God. Then, where are you? Uncreated, unforgiven, unloved, undone.

I Am Anne Frank

And the devil, a Monsignor, and conjoined twins. I am every character in every episode, a composite sketch of all of them. Her God, Anne's? Why, he left. Hitler gassed God too. A young girl forced to live in an attic and then betrayal. Is that your God, the one Hitler gassed and Nietzsche killed?

Suffice it to say, my god is not your God. My creator? See that shredder over there, the studio's shredder? That is my creator. That is why I look like this. What am I doing here? Well, simply, I was created here and it's damnably difficult to be anywhere else right now. I speak metaphorically, of course about the "I" thing. I know what you're thinking, a bit of a confusing mess.

Do I suffer? Do you? Of course, you do. Don't I look like one of Hieronymus Bosch's paintings, ghastly tangled up bodies skewered on great pikes and faces screaming agony beyond words, in greasy oil paints, hanging in a church to scare away both the spirits of the dead and the living? Briarcliff redux? Laugh and call me a cut up. I maintain I am a cut above, for I am all that ever was from the miseries that have come from the minds of Brad Falchuk and Ryan Murphy.

I am nothing like you, you're thinking. And what is like you, may I ask? Perfectly sane, healthy, living an ethical life, waiting for judgment day and the clarion call from Gideon? You have it all wrong. You certainly *are* like me. You see, I am that which is the end product of all the horror that Twentieth Century Fox Television has crammed into that hungry shredder over there.

You don't want to know, but there are some things about me that you haven't seen. On the cutting room floor, so to speak, me. Now I am an amalgam of all the suffering you have seen. Yet I am not different from you. Say again, you ask? I am not different from you.

You suffer; I suffer.

You're Canned!

It just so happens that all of what has been me will be dumped into that can over there that waits for ignominious burial at a land fill. We are all contingent, my friend. We exist from moment to moment. You cannot go back again to that time in little league where you hit the winning run.

You have memories. So do I. They are all here, jumbled in front of you. A bit of Ethel Darling, Elsa Mars, Gloria Mott. Wait, there's more, my masculine side: Jimmy Darling, Spalding, John Lowe. I'm all here, in here. So what am I all about? Suffering. What exactly do I mean? Sit back and don't stick your fingers in there or you will end up like me.

We are but contingent beings in a contingent universe. Contingent because we grow, grow old, think, dream, and then lose it all the moment when being ends. This is the real horror, no change at all: nothingness. Then why do you watch? Why watch the horror of the ending of a life? What does it mean to you? There but for the grace of God . . . There it is again, God.

Patients Committed Here Suffer Not Only Diseases of the Mind, but Also of the Body

So says Dr. Arden in episode 1 of Season Two. Whose god is their god? Who is the god of freaks, serial killers, the condemned who slobber and grimace and scream at voices that say, die, die, die. Who is the god of ghosts and specters and poltergeists? This is your god of love and compassion? Nietzsche is right, they have been feeding you nothing but crap on the notion of good and evil. They've sold you down the river just as they did me when they cut them up to make me. There is no god of good.

As a matter of fact, after this, you'll probably live forever. That's what Dr. Arden says to Shelly about the injection he as just given her after he has taken her legs (Season Two, episode 4). What do you think? Live forever, no legs? Suffering, all of it. How do we get to this point, this level of abject cruelty? Let's ask the Buddha.

The Buddha isn't born Buddha. He's born Siddhartha Gautama who is brought up a spoiled pampered prince. He gets anything he wants and his father keeps all the bad stuff away. He doesn't see freaks or the insane, only obedient servants and his family. There are no ghosts haunting his palace. He doesn't even get to go out and hurl projectiles at wild game like the other boys do. Boring, right?

Say you never saw Bette and Dot, could you ever imagine them? Of course not, because Daddy keeps all that away. What happens when you've been mollycoddled all your life? Well, Siddhartha, as all young men do, got in his mind that he wanted to disobey old Daddy and take a jaunt outside the palace. Took a faithful servant with him. You know who he took? Elsa Mars. Why her? He didn't know it yet but she was about to show him the freak show of freak shows. She showed him disease, old age, starvation, and death.

Suffering. So, what does this do to him? No, freak. He doesn't run right home and put on the telly to watch more suffering like you do. He doesn't stuff his mind on nasty hallucinations and conjoined twins whose mother just got trashed. He doesn't cling to his seat just waiting for Bloody Face to wield that ice pick. No, he walks out. Leaves home. Gone. Why? He simply can't understand this thing called suffering. That stuff that gets you all high and happy and makes your heart race. Get some exercise, couch potato. So, Siddhartha sets out to find this thing called suffering. He had to find it first, you see, before he could do anything about it.

What does he find? It's all around us, that's the point. It's everywhere. It's got to stop says Siddhartha. So where do you go to stop suffering? Turn the damn TV off. That's it; hit the button on the remote.

Sister Jude fights with the Devil. Okay, but so isn't everyone else at Briarcliff fighting something? Ding ding ding. Suffering. So what does Siddhartha do to shut down the proverbial death chute of suffering? He gets into meditation big time. So much so he begins to starve himself. Gets into that anorexia thing in a big way. His body starts eating his organs, that's how big into meditation and fasting he gets. He is suffering . . .

Sure, like Jesus, but in a different way. Jesus doesn't ask to be crucified, all he wants is to continue preaching. Remember, he is going to God anyway. Siddhartha has no god. Nope, none. He is on his own, a meditating fool. Then he realizes that he's just that, a fool. He's been looking for the origin of suffering and, shazam . . . there it is, him. He's become the poster child for suffering. So what does he do? What any other respecting mendicant would do, he sits under a tree.

Now, you might be thinking of the two bums in *Waiting for Godot*, waiting under a spindly tree for God to come by and save them from the sheer boredom of existence. Not Siddhartha. Nope, he picks the biggest damn tree in the province to sit under. There he is, skinnier than Gandhi, probably wearing the same kind of wrap that Gandhi did. Of course, he sits in a really good yoga pose. What does he do? He meditates. Oh, not that again . . . Deeper, deeper, deeper . . . For three watches of the night he meditates. What does he see? He watches every episode of *American Horror Story*—what you see before you now—me.

The freaks, the specters, the dead, the dying, the arm ripped out of its socket, the pain of schizophrenia all pass by him. He sees all his past lives and the lives of others. Death and rebirth over and over again. He sees the most wretched of beggars being reborn as kings. He sees kings being reborn as freaks without a mind at all, pinheads every one of them. Why all this reversal? Karma he calls it. If you cause suffering, watch out, your rebirth might be nasty. If you stop suffering, well maybe you will get a good rebirth sometime. When? Can't say.

So he sees it all. In remembering his past lives he sees a tiger, as emaciated as him with two skinny starving cubs. What does he do, shoot her and them to take them out of their misery? They're tigers, damn it. Killers of women and babies. No, he cuts himself. No, not like the cutters at Briarcliff. He does the big nasty on his arms like someone who wants to commit suicide. Momma tiger smells his blood and gobbles him up. Suffering? Beyond suffering. What the hell is Siddhartha thinking? Well, it's better that he suffers than the tiger because he knows he will be reborn and the tiger doesn't. Yeah, he gets a few attaboys from Dr. Karma and he's off on another round of rebirths. Sister Jude and Sister Mary Eunice, eat your hearts out. He's got places to go, places to be. Where the hell are you two going after Briarcliff? You won't be coming back. How boring.

Buddha is channeling Nietzsche, right, that eternal recurrence thing? No. Who the hell wants to eternally recur? You see that's special insight number two he gets—after the remembering of all past lives thing—that we suffer because we cling to things. You, sufferer, binge watcher of *American Horror Story* . . . Guess what, you're on that eternal recurrence track. Time to get off and get a life. So that's what Siddhartha does, he gets a better life. When he wakes up he's a Buddha like all the other Buddhas he has seen in his past lives tour. He sees he doesn't even have to cling to life. He sees that he can end the freak show routine as the skinniest man alive, and push the demons out of his head, yes, exorcise them, the way Sister Jude, Dr. Thredson, Father Howard, and the priest do to Jed.

He doesn't have a manual, biblical sayings, crosses, or holy water. Remember the Buddha has no god. He simply realizes that there is a chain of causes. You do bad things; worse things happen. Like Briarcliff. It goes from shoveling dead TB victims down the death chute to gathering together the criminally insane. Now how much worse can that get? Well, we see how much worse that thing gets with the devil getting involved.

The big Buddha insight is that we are contingent. Like me. Contingent, meaning that we are never the same from moment to moment. Take me, lose a clipping, gain a clipping. Here, take one. There, I'm still talking, right. Do I sound any different? No, of course not. So, empty the ash tray on me, go ahead. There, any different? You see? Maybe my voice is a bit more gravelly. Stuff reeks too.

Oh, by the way, you just changed. Don't look at me like that. You did. You have skin flakes falling from you, you breathed in air, maybe you farted. No, I am not being crude. You changed, you aren't the same as you were just moments ago. You are a thinking thing, remember? Are you playing just one endless loop of film in your head? No you are shredding it just like that monstrous thing over there. Shredding, re-sorting just like me.

Mara

Season Two, episode 13: Lana says, "You don't have any idea what I'm capable of."

> Says Jude, "Just remember, if you look in the face of evil, evil's gonna look right back at you."

We: "You, I, and the Buddha are about to look evil right in the face."

Back to the movie. Siddhartha, now Buddha, has ended his *American Horror Story*, last episode, series finale. Not so fast. You see, when he's sitting under the tree, a deva, well more like a demon, comes to be. His name is Mara. The worst. His name translates to death.

The moment that he sees that the Buddha is enlightened he turns on all the charm he has to cut that shit right the hell out of old Buddha. He sends his ogle-worthy daughters and a hundred other come-hithers to seduce him. He rides with an army of elephants to trample the Buddha. He tells the Buddha to die, die, die. The Buddha whisks him away. He changes channels. He goes to a heartwarming story on the movie network, not that garbage you've been watching. He turns off the suffering by becoming invisible to it. He disappears. He wears a cloak, not of many colors, but of no color at all. Mara, of course, is pissed, disappointed, but pissed. So Mara decides to go after all the Buddha's disciples.

It's Not Your Fault, Baby . . . It's Mine

Lana blows Johnny away, just like that (Season Two, episode 13). Sure, he's the son of Bloody Face. Can't a guy catch a break? Maybe a guy can. For that we need to get back to old Buddha.

I will back-track a bit. Like Jesus, the Buddha converts a whole bunch of folks to become, not disciples, but monks. Thousands of them. Like Jesus, he goes on tour, this place and that all across northern India. Then one day he is out walking alone. Guess what. He runs into Bloody Face.

You can't make this shit up. The guys at *American Horror Story* had to be watching reruns of old Buddha movies when they came up with this character. The Buddha is walking down the road alone when along comes this crazed man wielding a sword, a big-ass curved scimitar like you see in old genie-out-of-the-bottle movies. Well, and get this, he has a garland of fingers around his neck. Some say he has 999 fingers and is looking to get his even one thousand from the Buddha's own hand and life. Told you we would get to the fingers thing.

No, he wasn't called Bloody Face. Angulimala. Means garland of fingers. So, anyway, Angulimala has terrorized the countryside for years. Everyone hates him. So, what does the Buddha do? No he doesn't hold up the cross and tie a string of garlic around his neck. No stake in the heart; no exorcism. He simply uses his special power (he got by becoming Buddha) to keep just out of the way of Angulimala. Angulimala gets tired and stops. Angulimala then talks to the Buddha and the Buddha makes him a monk.

Huh? Yeah, somehow Angulimala has gone bad . . . that chain of causes thing again. A freak like Mara has gotten to him, cursed him and the only way he can lift the curse is to deliver to his freak a thousand fingers. Hey, he isn't a bad guy underneath it all. He just has to get out of the killing routine to realize it. What do you think? Do you think that Bloody Face was born a serial killer? Well the show seems to think so.

So, we have this Angulimala guy becoming a monk. Well the villagers all around don't know this. They are calling the king to account—get this Angulimala guy. The good king sets out with his posse and, what do you know, they find the Buddha with Angulimala. The king sees that Angulimala is now a good guy and gives up his crusade. The villagers don't believe this and beat up Angulimala. He deserves it? Sure, he does because he hasn't done anything to end *their* suffering, only his own. Nietzsche calls it *ressentiment*—hostility directed at someone that they can do nothing about—when Angulimala was a serial killer. As a monk, well he's a pacifist, an easy target. Hey, throw stones at that adulteress, why don't you? Yeah, you throw that first stone if you are so guiltless. Violence against violence, works every time . . .

Finally, the villagers get to vent the anger they have held pent up inside for so many years. Even after beating up Angulimala, they stay angry. You see, they can't let go. They suffer. They're going to die young because they can't let it go. Then they're going to be reborn again. I'd love to see how Dr. Karma does the villagers' rebirths. What a calculation. Who are they, really? They are the inmates in Briarcliff, wandering around listening to the foul voices of their past twisted lives, telling them to kill others, or simply go into convulsions as a way to end the pain.

Just Like Dad

So we have Bloody Face cut off Leo's arm in Season Two, episode 1, and in the last episode of the season, we have Johnny hacking off Leo's arm. So, is this a rebirth of the same? Is Bloody Face reborn as Johnny? Leo being reborn as Leo? What ghastly notion are we trying to cling to? Sorry Leo and Leo, cling is not the best term now, is it . . .

Okay, now what? you ask. Well, the Buddha says to his followers, stop clinging to that which is impossible to cling to. Stop clinging to the idea that you are a freak, insane, or possessed. Let it all go. You see, Buddha knows that he will not be reborn again. He's done with all that. When he dies, he dies. So, he breaks the chain and where does he go? Nobody knows, but the Buddha thinks it's a nirvana-like place. He's out of the horror show of suffering, gone, done.

Mara never stops harassing Buddha. Even when Buddha is on his death bed, he keeps trying to get the Buddha to die on Mara's terms. Buddha will have none of it. He simply slips into oblivion. So, are we done with Buddhas now? What do you think? Jews are still waiting for their messiah. Christ is supposed to return but he missed the train or something. Buddha said there would be more Buddhas.

We're all still waiting and Mara, well, like the Devil, he's still around. In fact, I saw his face just behind you there. Yeah, you who are binging Season Seven. Mara is encouraging you to watch the next episode. Let the kids eat leftovers, he's saying.

Me, well you know my fate. I'll be around for a while, and then I will be gone. I leave Mara with you. Take good care of him. Me, leave like the Buddha? Gone to a better place? It's a garbage dump. Guess who is getting reborn . . . Nietzsche, just get off my ass, will you . . . ?

12
A Month from Now, I'll Be a Balding, Toothless Skeleton

SETH M. WALKER

You slowly and deliberately walk in, squinting through the smoky haze as you make your way to the bar. The smell of cheap liquor and stale nuts cuts through the tide of pretentious young men. The jukebox is playing some old, boring hit of years past. You know you're in the right place.

Watching the predatorial gazes of these men lust after everyone in sight, you start to realize something is different tonight. The slow bat of your eyes and the coy blush you've been flaunting hasn't turned any heads. The trivial banter and purposeful drinks you're used to aren't coming your way either. They aren't noticing *you*.

It feels good to get noticed in public—to turn heads, capture alluring gazes . . . incite lustful, passionate desires. Well, at least for someone teetering a bit too close to the narcissistic edge of the cliff like Fiona Goode. And it's easy for people like her to get used to this sort of thing. But, imagine how you'd feel if all of a sudden there was a shift in this usual pattern. Even worse, imagine this shift occurred alongside a terminal diagnosis: not only has your sexual prowess taken a drastic turn, so has your health.

Fiona might not be the *nicest* of the modern-day Coven of witches hanging out in New Orleans, but she's certainly one of the *hardest* and most cutthroat. And putting ourselves in her position—suddenly dealing with such devastating circumstances and angst—might help us understand what she's going through a bit better: feeling like you're withering away while seeing those around you filled with vitality and youthful beauty is tough—especially when it's more than just *feeling* like you're withering away.

A common thread among Fiona and other characters throughout *Coven* is resistance to change. And one of the great Eastern-cum-Western religious traditions, Buddhism, takes this as one of its main starting points as well. Buddhist philosophy locates destructive "thirsts" and "cravings" as the root of our suffering. Getting rid of that suffering depends on addressing those destructive patterns of behavior that leave us feeling so miserable. On the show, the outcomes of these behaviors are typically obvious (and usually aren't as great as they're intended to be). But, framing these situations in terms of Buddhist philosophy helps unravel a bit more of the details we might be glossing over as we sit back and enjoy the show over a warm, hearty, fish-head gumbo. And they're details that are clearly relevant outside of the series too.

You've Been Fading

At the beginning of "The Replacements," we see Fiona scrambling around in the middle of the night for her medications. A flashback to 1971 helps us understand what's *really* on her mind. Before murdering the reigning Supreme (the leading generational witch gifted with *all* of the possible powers rather than just one or a few), Anna-Leigh Leighton, in order to take her place, Fiona pulls various pill bottles out of her leader's purse, making it clear she knows exactly what's going on:

> They say when a new Supreme starts to flower, the old Supreme begins to fade. You've been fading, Anna-Leigh . . . You're weak, Anna-Leigh. We both know why: diabetes, heart trouble, liver failure—God knows what else. As I get stronger, you get weaker.

We can imagine, then, that Fiona's memory of that night is haunting her as its familiarity becomes troubling. Fiona is now the one *fading*, and she knows it. We see her out at a bar shortly after this opening sequence, getting overlooked by those she'd normally and effortlessly attract. The only eye she's catching is her own: an inner, critical eye, filled with disappointment and sadness because of the state she's in.

Fiona obviously hasn't been the only one to ever notice this natural and upsetting lifelong progression. The Buddha, tradition tells us, came to this realization as well: all life is suffering. The Pali term for this is *dukkha*, and it actually captures a bit more than the usual English translation of "suffering," which can also confusingly frame Buddhist teachings as strangely pessimistic rather than *realistic*: it can certainly be viewed in this basic, "ordinary" sort of way (like how it feels to get hit in the back by a voodoo-summoned zombie), but it also extends to change and conditionality.

The understanding that everything is both in constant flux and a cause and an effect of something else is foundational in Buddhist philosophy. And it sounds fairly obvious when you consider these kinds of ideas. But, it's not as easy to *live* them as it might seem. Problems start to arise when we cling to things as if they are static and unchanging. Fighting against the inherent conditions of the world doesn't usually go well, and the Coven at Miss Robichaux's Academy has a hard time casting their powers to the side so this can happen.

We Rot. We Die.

One of the most important aspects of *dukkha* is that everything in the world is in constant flux. The Buddha recognized this *anicca*, or "impermanence," and pointing this out served as the backbone for his teachings. Fiona's constant awareness of this taking place throughout the season—from watching her hair fall out from chemotherapy to noticing the younger witches at Miss Robichaux's Academy grow stronger and manifest new powers—results in all sorts of misguided and selfish attempts to halt this change and reverse the process. But, perhaps the most obvious indication of the source of her inner turmoil from all of this change and conditionality is her equation of beauty and youth.

From her barroom excursions to her fixation on physical appearance, Fiona is dangerously obsessed. When she took Madison Montgomery out for drinks one night, we watched Fiona's sullen reaction as Madison stole all of the attention from the men around them. "My life force is literally pouring out of my body and into yours," she tells Madison near the end of the episode ("The Replacements"). And Fiona is *not* ready for this to happen. But, it's this subtle indication again of beauty and youth going hand-in-hand that frames the sort of suffering she deals with throughout the season.

When her new serial-killing lover, the Axeman, suggests the two of them run away together to live out the rest of her days in each other's company without any other worries, she tells him that she doesn't want him watching her decay and wither away. It's not the dying she's scared of; it's the thought that someone will watch her crumble. "You are beautiful," he tells her. "You're just a fool in love," she responds. "You like the way I look? Take a picture. A month from now, I'll be a balding, toothless skeleton" ("The Sacred Taking"). It's a shame the medical researcher she's been funding, David, isn't around anymore to give Fiona another blunt reminder, maybe actually shaking her from her ignorance this time: "We are organic matter. We are animals. We rot. We die" ("Bitchcraft").

The Selfish Detours I've Taken

Failing to understand the "constant pain and ugliness" that Fiona notes as what's most troubling ("The Sacred Taking") leaves her constantly wanting more and never being truly happy. "You've lived the big life," the Axeman tells her. "You went everywhere, you met everyone. You've done everything that your stony little heart desires. But you're never ever truly happy, huh?" ("Protect the Coven").

This constant leap from one fleeting satisfaction to the next is also a major part of our ever-present *dis*satisfaction, the Buddha taught. Our insatiable thirsts (*taṇhā*) leave us in a state similar to Fiona: never truly being satisfied or happy. In the so-called "Fire Sermon," the Buddha likened our thirsts to a fire that never goes out—the flames spreading from one place to the next, lapping up everything they touch and never being fully quenched. In "Setting the Wheel of Dhamma in Motion," the Buddha distinguished between different types of thirsts: sense pleasures (*kāma*), existence (*bhava*), and non-existence, or the annihilation of negative and undesirable states (*vibhava*). And *Coven* gives us a great depiction of each.

We've already seen how Fiona's lifelong escapades and thirst for *kāma* have left her: in a run-down, solemn state, realizing how empty her life has been. We see a great example of this taking place with Madame Delphine LaLaurie near the end of the season as well. At the beginning of "Protect the Coven," when Delphine slaughters a chicken for dinner, the blood spurting out of its headless form draws her fascination. We can almost *feel* her intrigue as she fingers the life-force seeping out of its neck. Shortly after, we also get to see how this chicken-head-chopping spearheaded the grotesque new hobby that ultimately sealed her fate (literally, in a coffin). When one of her slaves injures himself in the attic, bleeding out all over the floor, Delphine slowly approaches, reaching down to stick her hand into the open, gushing wound across his leg. After pulling her dripping fingers back to admire, she knocks him unconscious and strings him up from the ceiling to bleed him out.

Well, fast-forward over 150 years later to an injured groundskeeper at Miss Robichaux's Academy and we see a little Delphine *déjà vu*. Some chloroform and an empty attic (sans the creepy, antique dolls and tea sets . . . what's going on, Spalding?!), and Delphine is on her way to torturing and bleeding out her first victim in almost two centuries.

But, it didn't really go as planned. When Spalding's ghost suddenly appears among the dolls as she finishes gutting and filleting the groundskeeper, he tells her he's been watching her live her life without purpose (even in death, he apparently can't stop being a creeper!). "I thought I'd found my purpose, or at least a hobby," she solemnly confesses to him. "Mostly, I think I just made a mess" ("Protect the Coven"). Just like Fiona, Delphine has been clinging to these fleeting satisfactions (which are, clearly, a bit more gruesome than the philandering and world traveling Fiona's been attracted to) that have remained both insatiable and destructive (and incredibly messy).

While *kāma* appears throughout the season in a few other ways as well—such as relational attachment among the characters—*bhava* and *vibhava* are responsible for most of the angst and dissatisfaction we see among the witches.

I Want That Drug, David, and I Want It Now

The annihilation of negative and undesirable states sounds fairly self-explanatory, but in extreme instances, it can also manifest as *self*-annihilation, or, suicide. Though no one in the Coven really seems to express it like that, and at one point, we see Fiona reject it completely. When the Axeman asks her if she's ever considered stopping her natural decay and suffering on her own, she responds, "I wouldn't give anyone the satisfaction of me killing myself. I'll stay alive just to spite them" ("The Sacred Taking"). Her hardened and vindictive personality obviously leaves little room for a hasty departure of this world, no matter how negative and undesirable the state she's in.

Not wanting to be in an undesirable state (like persistent physical decay) and wanting to *be* in every positive way imaginable (young, beautiful, full of energy and appeal) clearly go hand-in-hand. And Fiona's thirst for perpetual beauty and vitality—for *existence*—fuels the fire burning those around her. In the first episode ("Bitchcraft"), Fiona tells David that she wants a new experimental drug he's developing: a healing serum called RM47. After seeing the dramatic and miraculous effects the serum has on a previously-terminal monkey named Allegra (her kidneys were failing), Fiona flirtatiously tells David, "I'll have what she's having." When David tells her that she needs to wait another two years for human trials to begin and instead suggests cosmetic surgery to help satisfy her desire for a more youthful appearance, she responds, "What I need is an infusion of vitality—of youth. I want that drug, David, and I want it now." And, as we all know, Fiona isn't exactly the only one in New Orleans consumed by these thirsty flames.

I'll Have What She's Having

Coven opens in 1834 New Orleans with Delphine literally smearing blood all over her face and neck to try to keep a youthful appearance. "When the blood dries," she tells her husband, staring at her through the mirror in a bewildered gaze, "my skin's supposed to be tight as a drum. Just look at this waddle" ("Bitchcraft"). The poultice was made from a human pancreas—specifically harvested from the slaves she kept in her attic's torture chamber. Possessing a vanity on par with Ms. Goode, Delphine's use of expensive creams from Europe and this sickening concoction displays the harmful measures that can be taken by those fully absorbed by their cravings and attachments. Her selfish desires obviously get the best of her.

Delphine does sort of reveal that her thirst for youth and beauty is out of control: "You think I want to do this?" she asks her daughter. "You can blame your father and his fresh-faced whore." When Marie Laveau learns that one of the victims in Delphine's playhouse of horrors was her lover, Bastien, she tricks Delphine into drinking a love potion that will supposedly keep her husband's interest on her and not his much younger mistresses. After falling unconscious, Delphine wakes to discover her entire family had been killed by Marie and that she didn't exactly drink a love potion. The *immortality* potion would keep Delphine alive to wallow in the eternal suffering she would face, bound, gagged, and sealed in a buried coffin not far from her home.

This was an interesting twist in the story for us, too: typically, immortality is thought about as a *good* thing (contrary to the thirst for existence the Buddha cautioned against, of course). I guess it depends on how you would be spending those eternal days that makes all the difference—and being chained and buried underground in solitude is not a very comforting thought or the way we'd probably want to live. When the Coven discovers Delphine's resting place in present-day New Orleans, and when Fiona later returns to uncover her ("Boy Parts"), we're met with more than a 150-year-old waft of BO (though that's certainly there too!). Delphine is a living example of what Fiona could be as well: resistant to physical deterioration—life without the prospect of slowly withering away. If she can't *naturally* stop her mortal decay and halt the impermanence of this world, then perhaps it's time to try something else.

I Sold My Soul to Papa Legba

Realizing that Marie has still been around this whole time as well, Fiona takes a stroll across town to the beauty salon she owns (there's some not-so-subtle irony here I hope you're catching) to see what's been keeping her alive for so long. "I want what you have," Fiona tells her. "Whatever it is that has kept you young all these years." Fiona is quite literally laughed out of the shop (not before setting a few things on fire, of course): "Oh, that is rich!" Marie replies. "You could offer me a unicorn that shit hundred dollar bills and I'd still never give you more than a headache" ("Boy Parts").

Well, we figure out a little later in the season ("The Magical Delights of Stevie Nicks") that Marie's own thirst for life (*bhava*) resulted in her making a tricky pact with Papa Legba, an intermediary between the world of the dead and the world of the living (who also has a fond appreciation for fine cocaine); *Coven* generally depicts him as a stand-in for the Christian "devil," maintaining personal "hells" for each of the characters.

Marie has actually been hanging around the block for over 300 years, thanks to Mr. Legba. But, as we discover, it's not the *healthiest* relationship. "You can help me live, Marie,"

Fiona pleads later in the season ("The Magical Delights of Stevie Nicks"). "You know the secret—you gave it to that despicable, torturing racist." It's not that simple, though: if Marie gives Fiona the same potion (actually, a vial of her tears), then Fiona wouldn't exactly *heal* and regain her vitality; she'd be stuck in an endless loop of pain and partial decay. "Who gave it to *you*?" Fiona then asks. "I don't think you're ready for that," Marie responds. "Tell me your secret," Fiona continues. "I sold my soul to Papa Legba." In this case, we learn, it was Marie's pregnancy and fixation on *new* life that had her longing for a way out of the cosmic sequence of birth and death. Every year, Papa Legba visits her to collect an innocent life per the arrangement of the sale. The first year, it was Marie's own baby. And hundreds of others have lost their young lives because of Marie's own thirst for existence.

Is that enough to turn Fiona off to the idea of some devilish assistance in achieving the same thing? Not a chance. And not long after her conversation with Marie, Fiona summons the lurking, coked up, soul-hungry bargainer for an arrangement of her own. Surprisingly, it doesn't really take much effort either (though the four lines of cocaine Fiona meticulously prepared in advance probably didn't hurt). Fiona gets right to the point when he arrives: "I don't want to die." "I give you my soul, and what do you give me in return?" she asks. "Freedom from death," he replies. "Life everlasting, no aging, no decrepitude, forever," she bargains. And just like that, along with certain *services* provided to him once each year—something like crippling her own daughter (Fiona says she'd do it today) or murdering an innocent person ("Whatever it takes!" she tells him)—they've got a deal. But, one tiny problem: when they try to make the exchange and solidify the pact, Mr. Legba realizes Fiona doesn't have a soul, and the deal is off. And there's not enough cocaine in the world to convince him otherwise.

We can easily get lost in a philosophical mess if we dive too deep into this idea of "no soul" or "non-self"—what the Buddha referred to as *anatta*—but it's enough for our purposes here to say that the false sense of a separate, individual "self" is part of the misunderstanding driving our thirsts and attachments. The idea that we're separate and distinct (and can be *preserved*) runs in the face of the impermanent reality the Buddha taught: just as everything around us is in constant flux, so are *we* and the various components that make us *us*. Nothing is static, and nothing is *permanent*—not even us, and certainly not some immaterial, abstract construct of self or soul. So, while Papa Legba's remark might sound like a *negative* assessment of Fiona, we might actually consider it an insightful way out of her suffering in disguise. Too bad she didn't heed that shady druggie's words of wisdom.

I'll Just Kill 'Em All

But, potions, serums, supernatural coke addicts, and even literally sucking the life-force out of other people (sorry, David, but thank you for your years of service . . .) were never Fiona's only options for stalling the inevitable. The *problem*, she repeatedly revisits when these other solutions don't seem to work out, is that there's a new Supreme on the rise. And that's how things work: as a new one rises, the former slowly fades. But, if there's no new Supreme nudging her off her macabre throne, then she wouldn't have anything to worry about. Right?

When Fiona gets the feeling that her replacement might be Madison, she slits her throat in a scene reminding us of Fiona's murder of Anna-Leigh ("The Replacements"). Granted, Fiona does try to persuade Madison to kill *her* first, but hey, ya snooze, ya lose. The same thing happens with Nan in "The Magical Delights of Stevie Nicks." When she tells Fiona she thinks she might be the new Supreme, Fiona and Marie drown her in a bathtub, killing two birds with one stone: remove the source of her agony and appease Mr. Legba for Marie with a *mostly* innocent life (just grab one of those cliché brooms we all expected to see this season and sweep Luke's mother's death under the rug). But, as we all know, even these types of attempts aren't enough to appease those burning flames of desire—nor the natural cycle of life.

Just Look at this Waddle

But, trying to halt or stop the process of change—and even bringing people back to life—is not the solution the Buddha taught. It only stalls the inevitable, and more importantly, it doesn't relieve us of our inner turmoil: we're always kept longing for more—fueling the fire as it slowly consumes us. The Buddha and his later commentators emphasized the practice of mindfulness—in quiet meditation and throughout one's daily life. This amounts to a deep awareness of *everything*. Cultivating it might start with simply paying attention to your own internal thoughts and physical changes, but it gradually extends to understanding the impermanence and connectivity of the world around you as well.

The canonical teachings of the Buddha (*suttas*) encourage his followers to contemplate the inner workings and mechanics of the body to help relieve thirsts and attachments. Contemplating "foulness" is particularly instructive in this case. In the *Girimananda Sutta*, the Buddha reminds one of his attendants that our bodies are composed of many different *foul* things—like bones, organs, bile, snot, pus, blood, sweat, spit, feces, and urine. Contemplating the makeup of the human body in this way is a great reality check on the nature of things—it also might make it a bit more difficult to unhealthily lust after someone else (*kāma*) or long to preserve oneself (*bhava*) if all you see is an outer shell filled with blood, bile, and pus.

A famous fifth-century commentator on the Buddha's teachings, Buddhaghosa, elaborates on this type of contemplative practice in the *Visuddhimagga* ("The Path of Purification") by extending it to a meditation on the states of different types of corpses (like those that are bloated, festering, or worm infested). The idea here is to become mindfully aware of the natural process of decomposition and decay. Buddhaghosa is just driving the Buddha's points home by telling his readers, "Hey, this is what happens: we're going to die, we're going to decay, we're going to rot, and we should be so lucky if mounds of worms and maggots decide to repurpose our bloated, festering flesh for a weekend brunch. Nothing is static, and all is susceptible to change." Sounds a little familiar, too, huh? (*cough*, David).

Just a Woman Facing the Inevitable

As a new, reinvigorated Coven emerges under Cordelia Foxx's rule (aside from being Fiona's daughter, she was apparently the rising Supreme this whole time as well!), a shriveled Fiona bids us a final farewell. The two of them have one last mother-daughter conversation that ends with an exchange of wisdom on the nature of life, death, and mindfulness that we probably weren't expecting ("The Seven Wonders").

During those last few moments of Fiona's life, Cordelia asks her if she was always so awful to her because she knew that one day she'd take away her power. "You took my power the minute I gave birth to you," a fading Fiona replies. "A woman becomes a mother, she can't help but see her mortality in that cherubic little face. Every time I looked at you, I saw my own death. You were a constant reminder of my worst fears."

Fiona pleads with Cordelia to end her suffering and offers her a dagger (though Fiona's track record with these types of one-on-one confrontations isn't too reassuring). "You're scared. Maybe for the first time in your life," Cordelia tells her.

> No powers. No magic. Just a woman facing the inevitable. A divine being finally having a human experience. No one can help you, mother. You have to do this alone. And the only way out is through. So feel the fear, and the pain. Let it all in, and then let it all go.

By the end of the season, it was obviously a little too late to start encouraging Fiona to mindfully meditate on the nature of her existence. But, Cordelia's passing wisdom may be an indication that it's not too late for the remaining witches at Miss Robichaux's Academy—and the multitude of new recruits. Since those still left—Cordelia, Zoe, Queenie, and

Kyle—all had unique experiences with death and the comings and goings of life (we might even consider Zoe's body-part-assembly of Kyle to be a meditation of sorts on death), perhaps they've developed a keen awareness of how to positively navigate this confusing, burning terrain that can be passed on to the new generation of witches.

We can only speculate, but I think we can assume that it's at least a lot more likely under Cordelia's rule than it was under Fiona's.

13
Burn the Witch!

CHERISE HUNTINGFORD

Did she make you cry
Make you break down
Shatter your illusions of love?

—Fleetwood Mac, "Gold Dust Woman"

When Zoe Benson loses her virginity in a climax of her beau's blood, the scene can't help but evoke the infamous *vagina dentata* legend; a genetic affliction of the female genitalia whereby a nasty set of nether-gnashers threatens castration of would-be suitors.

The folktale is an extreme version of the *femme fatale*—typecast as the antagonist; a strong, sexually aggressive woman who seduces only to destroy, and must be punished for her domination and destruction of the male hero.

And then *American Horror Story*, as is its MO, twists the convention—and turns it in a black-clad, fiercely feminist direction.

In *Coven's* less toothy, though just as fatal, iteration of the centuries-old *vagina dentata* myth, Zoe becomes the heroine, both embodying and subverting the archetype of the *femme fatale*. Before her cherry-popper has even cooled, Zoe doesn't allow the dry-spell her love life will inevitably suffer make her the stereotypical victim, nor does she let it detract from the business of bitchcraft; instead—in a Grand Guignol moment almost impossible to wipe clean from memory—she utilizes her pseudo man-eater to brain-burst her roommate's rapists, harnessing her preternatural power to rid the world (or at least the Kappa Lambda Gamma frat house) of the real *bad guys.*

But . . . black widow retribution is short-lived; when the cops come calling, Zoe freaks out—giving herself up along with the whole of Miss Robichaux's Academy. Reigning Supreme and "baddest witch in the whole damn town" Fiona Goode sums up Zoe's problem in a pithy assessment:

"You're soft. You're emotional."

While her "killer vagina" chews up and hocks out pop culture's fallaciously phallic, astride-a-broomstick wet dream of the witchy woman (who beguiles with supernatural sex appeal and bedroom magic—not aneurysms), the revealed ambiguity of Zoe's character reminds us that as much as she's a bona fide badass, purebred witch—she's also *still just a girl*.

You Haven't Walked in My Shoes—or Ridden My Broom

The witch, in fictional narratives and in history, is almost always a woman. There is a male counterpart, but it's not the incarnation our minds conjure when we hear the word. The third season of *American Horror Story* uses our presupposition of that ancient figure to create a contemporary feminist metaphor: the members of a coven—or in this case, an academy for the descendants of Salem's "gifted"—stand apart from others of their sex; a combination of their inherited powers and expanding occultic enlightenment enable them to firmly plant a pointed boot upon patriarchy in all its guises.

It's a messy triumph, however; and not without a weighty price to be paid—although historically, this is not an unfamiliar scenario for women—witches or otherwise.

Around the time when the first whispers of "witch" were susurrating through European villages and towns like a poisoned wind, and the gallows tree was etching its silhouette into a portentous sky, thirteenth-century philosopher and Catholic priest Thomas Aquinas (1225–1274) proposed that there was a human universal nature, knowable by reason, existing to rightly order our desires. This "Natural Law" theory has since enjoyed an illustrious career, a favored invocation as "proof" against both individuals and groups challenging anachronistic religious ordinances—including those defying the patriarchal institution of the Church.

Checking all the boxes, accused witches, with a suspected power all their own, would certainly have fallen beneath the hammer of Natural Law's judgment. Today, it's an *allegorical* sisterhood of mighty witches that stands as Natural Law's sublime antithetical counterpoint.

A distaste and distrust for the witches' *unnaturalness* is certainly a rampant sentiment amongst the "normal" characters of *Coven*: Zoe's own mother sends her to be sequestered ("*Coven*: Bitchcraft") rather than deal with—presumably—the shame and social fallout her daughter's hereditary curse will bring; Misty is barbecued in the Bayou by holy rollin' snake wranglers when she lets slip her resurgent ability ("*Coven*: Bitchcraft"); and, possibly the most *palpable* of examples: the academy's homely next-door neighbour brings Hell-fire in a housecoat, subjecting her son to a Comet-enema so that he may purged of the young witches' unclean influence ("*Coven*: The Sacred Taking").

Even the Coven's moral compass personified, Cordelia, courts an unspoken suspicion upon her failure to conceive—*is it the result of some righteous, divine judgment?* She is, after all, a witch.

But in contrast to those who perpetuate a rigid notion of what is "natural" (and in so doing manipulate fears of the "unnatural" to maintain discriminative status quos), philosopher Kyle Cupp protests the idea of "natural" being hemmed in by a culturally-bound set of parameters, or apparent biological imperatives.

He suggests that the intended interpretation of "natural" in Natural Law is ontological—it has to do with the nature of *being:* as rational *beings*, we are naturally inclined to seek knowledge, strive for freedom, and exercise free choice so that we may preserve and enhance our wellbeing—to not merely stay alive but to *live*.

As creatures with unprecedented cognition, self-awareness, and existential concerns, *these* are our natural ends. So, while this version of "natural" is distinctive to our entire species, the way in which the pursuit of knowledge, freedom, and free choice plays out for each of us follows a unique trajectory. That which is "natural" with regard to human motivation is thus an accumulation of abstractions, and "nature" refers then to our inner world, or identity—what is essentially an ever-changing, prone-to-turmoil construct.

Don't Make Me Kill the Frog

"When witches don't fight, we burn," warns Coven Supreme, Fiona, as she instructs her protégés on the perils of hiding their powers and pleading pacifist to those outside the Academy gates ("*Coven*: Bitchcraft").

Her words emphasise that there is no sanctuary in playing it safe—they also point to the scales of loss being fixed in equilibrium: whether they choose to "fight," or to immolate themselves for what they are, there will be sacrifice involved. Despite the fact that the prevailing oppressive authorities in *Coven* are homogenously, conspicuously male—from the Delphi Trust witch killers to the shot-calling uber-deity Papa Legba (to whom even immortal Voodoo Queen Marie Laveau and serial killer Delphine LaLaurie must bend), Fiona's certain prediction doesn't just sum up the fate foisted upon the witches by the ruling gender; the *biggest* war is within themselves, struggling against their dual natures of witch and woman. Because of this, they are immersed in a conflict for which there is no clear-cut victory.

As the Coven sisters battle against those external forces bearing upon them to submit to the stake, so too do they fight against succumbing to the trappings of their feminine nature. Once-burned, once-buried-alive, swamp-dwelling Misty, who resurrects 'gators to despatch her enemies and—*screw magic*—prefers an old-fashioned fist-to-face throw-down to settle scores in the (sister)'hood, happens to be fatally sensitive; during the trial of *descensum*, in which the witches vying for the "Supreme" title must astral travel into the afterlife's underworld, she can't distance herself from the projected hell of killing a hapless creature long enough to get back to reality, and her soft heart inevitably traps her in an eternity of frog vivisection ("*Coven*: The Seven Wonders"). Fiona also winds up in her own gender-specific Hades; waking to the stink of catfish and the cloying odor of domesticated life, the toppled matriarch realizes that her ever-after is the endless, looping horror of an axe murderer's hard-ons and knotty pine ("*Coven*: The Seven Wonders").

Playing house is not Fiona's only anathema distinctive to her being a woman; throughout the show she channels Snow White sorceress Evil Queen (except her magic mirror is clouded with coke), obsessed with the degeneration of her youth and dissipating vitality—to the point of murder, and at the expense of the relationship with her daughter, Cordelia: in the final (and first) embrace with her grown child, the refrain of Fiona's swansong is not so much regret as it is the self-revelation that becoming a mother has exposed her own mortality ("*Coven*: The Seven Wonders").

There *is* the affliction of maternal pangs, too—Cordelia puts the Coven's reputation at risk by enlisting its old rival, Voodoo priestess Marie Laveau, to help her conceive ("*Coven*: The Replacements"), while soon after, in an ironic parallel, her own distant mother is moved to revive a stranger's stillborn ("*Coven*: Burn, Witch. Burn!"). Socialite-cum-serial killer Madame Marie Delphine LaLaurie, who bats no lash at disembowelling, disfiguring, and dismembering slaves, is plagued by remorse for her mistreatment of her children; the realization of her atrocities is made acutely visceral as she encounters the reanimated corpse of a long-dead daughter—who, in an ineffably twisted affirmation of the biological bond, retains an instinctual recognition of her murderess mother—as Delphine contemplates her fall from high station, no longer lady of the manor but reincarnated as a chambermaid, her docile acceptance references a penance to be paid for her bad mothering, not the more likely karmic atonement for having butchered servants in a previous life ("*Coven*: Burn, Witch. Burn!").

Even would-be protagonist and rapist-slayer Zoe isn't exempt from her female "flaws," dubbed "soft" and swayed by emotion—an Achilles heel that compels her to bring back a frat boy from the dead ("*Coven*: Boy Parts"), and then fall in love with the reconstituted zombie.

Conversely; while womanhood makes dedication to the Coven complicated, their reputation as witches makes things difficult for the characters to be "regular" women: after lodging a couple of blessed silver bullets in brains around town, Cordelia's husband is unmasked as a witch hunter, who's been using his marriage to the academy's principal to build up his hit list ("*Coven*: The Magical Delights of Stevie Nicks"); and of course, Zoe's ungodly mutation holds the threat of death for any swain who dares enter its maw.

From Cupp's relativist perspective on nature's definition, Natural Law, rather than existing as a universally applicable method for "proper" behavior, instead encapsulates the *complexity* of utilizing "nature" as a governing force: reflecting the real-world ambiguity of the feminist experience, *Coven*'s supernaturally-imbued characters must continually negotiate between the opposing needs of their double natures—their innate identity as "woman," or their intrinsic power that contradicts the social construction of femininity.

We're All Wicked, Here

Influenced by Aristotle's *eudaimonism*—the moral philosophy that "right" action or behavior is that which promotes a person's essential wellbeing—and shaped by Christian theology, Aquinas's conception of Natural Law is grounded on the universal tenet that true (Godly) happiness can only be achieved by abandoning *evil* and pursuing *good.*

Given then the connotative associations of those eternal adversaries "good" and "evil," along with all that "natural" implies (and from the typically prejudiced psyche's perspective, all that it *doesn't*)—in the context of *Coven*, the idea of Natural Law seems a logical opposition to the show's supernatural feminist metaphor.

But faced with the possibility of a duality of resident natures (woman, witch, maybe more), Natural Law loses its moral high ground; it cannot act as a prescriptive set of rights and wrongs because—since in Aquinas's logic what is *natural* is "good"—multiple natures imply multiple moralities. Discord is inevitable.

Yet suppose variant natures could co-exist, and still pursue some broader constant of "good"? The sticking point is that not all needs are compatible with our so-called "natural ends"—our very desires can inhibit our own nature(s). Pathology is as much a part of the phenomenological as the drive to be a better person. We often take pleasure in destruction—even our own. Sometimes a witch is just plain wicked. Sometimes, the rest of the world is worse.

Although *American Horror Story's* oeuvre is a buffet of the *overt* brand of evil—skin-crawling, grisly, or unearthly—*Coven*'s black magic and its talismans are just a titillating veneer for an infinitely layered subtext, with the metaphorical witch pariah exposing a seemingly prosaic and familiar, yet far more insidious, bogeyman.

The most elemental definition of "evil" is anything that opposes "good": in the flipside universe of *American Horror Story*'s making, the *witches* are the vigilantes, and by pitting such figures whose mythos is swathed in superstitious dread against a greater antagonist—the oppressive male—*Coven* deconstructs conventional notions of "good" and "evil"; and functions as a bold commentary on what *really* constitutes malevolence.

Coven plays host to an array of set pieces parading the evil of misogyny—vicious, violent acts against women: not only does the Axeman have a penchant for making victims of females ("*Coven*: The Axeman Cometh"); so do Misty's hillbilly killers ("*Coven*: Bitchcraft"), the band of college rapists ("*Coven*: Bitchcraft"), and Cordelia's moonlighting witch-hunter husband.

When the men aren't direct perpetrators, they're harbingers of bad news, symbolic of their inherent threat: the police officers interrogating Zoe and Madison ("*Coven*: Boy Parts"), the doctor delivering Fiona's cancer prognosis and the one dispensing Cordelia's infertility verdict ("*Coven*: The Replacements").

This *is* a story about the strength of the feminine, however; and as a matter of course, the witches tend to get their own back—occasionally with relish. And where male characters aren't necessarily *bad,* the narrative itself takes a derisive dig, crippling them with an essential impotence; Zoe's brain damaged, undead paramour, Kyle, is little more than the academy "guard dog," only to be promoted to the prized position of butler when his predecessor, the pitiable, spurned Spalding, takes a mysterious leave of absence to play with his dolls ("*Coven*: The Axeman Cometh"); effete Witches' Council member Quentin Fleming is but an occasional campy diversion, and baby-faced boy-next-door Luke is recipient of the ultimate shame (the Comet-enema).

Marie Laveau's strapping lover, Bastien, is not exempt from emasculation, either; slave-owner Delphine achieves her creative apotheosis by transforming the terrified manservant into a half-witted, half-beast Minotaur ("*Coven*: Bitchcraft") (befittingly, this mythical monster represents *coincidentia oppositorum*, or meeting of opposites: the dichotomy of our higher rationality and our primordial, beastly nature—good versus evil).

There's another way *Coven* challenges the presumption of what determines "good" and "evil"—*both* appear to reside within female characters, encapsulating the moral grey area in which the women exist. In so doing, the absolutism of "good" and "evil" breaks down—context blurs the boundary between the moral and immoral, and within the grey, there is only a "hierarchy" of moral rightness—or wrongness.

There's no appealing to our greater sense of perspective when Kyle's grieving mother demonstrates an obscene perversion of "motherly" love at their reunion ("*Coven*: The Replacements")—yet the abusive mother is a recurrent motif in the show, and, as in Delphine's rending encounter with her revenant daughter, or Fiona's dying affirmation that despite everything, she did love Cordelia in her "own way" ("*Coven*: The Seven Wonders")—we feel empathy for at least *some* of its culprits.

In a less ambiguous instance; amidst a crimson rain of knife blows, an earlier generation of academy witches continue to exact frenzied revenge upon the murderer Axeman—long after he's paid the mortal price ("*Coven*: The Axeman Cometh"). The shadow of their sadistic pleasure looms large, but we allow the girls this brief departure into deviance because in *this* case, the Axeman is the bigger evil.

The trouble with drawing a line between "good" and "evil," and, as Natural Law theory dictates, using them as a categorical polarity to align our inclinations with our "virtuous" true natures, is that it is in our *nature* to be both good *and* evil.

Aquinas's antecessor Augustine (A.D. 354–430), from whom the Natural Law theorist inherited a sizeable philosophical patrimony, states in his autobiography *The Confessions*, "Things that exist are good." If something exists, then it possesses some degree of goodness—presumably because we can infer a creator behind existence, and in theological thinking, a creator points to God, who embodies "goodness." From this claim, Augustine argues that we can divide all existing things into two categories: the incorruptible and the corruptible. If something is incorruptible, it cannot be made worse; it cannot lose its intrinsic goodness. Yet being corruptible does not suggest an absence of goodness—to the contrary, if something can be made worse, there is the implication that it has goodness to lose.

Under Augustine's claim, because we exist, we retain an element of "good"—and our uniquely human corruptibility does not refute that truth. It is our very corrupt nature which confirms, however attenuated, the presence of goodness.

Yet Do I Fear Thy Nature

American Horror Story isn't the first to mess with femininity and dismantle the gender power structure—Shakespeare did it in spades: *As You Like It*'s Rosalind, who cuts ties with the paternal purse-strings, roughs it in the forest, and revels in screwing with her suitor Orlando's own sexual identity by posing as a man; Portia, who, besting wily Shylock (in *The Merchant of Venice*), usurps the role of protagonist from her lesser-witted male love interest; Cordelia, who leads an army to rescue her immured father, *King Lear*; and *Cleopatra*, Queen of the Nile, naval commander, and the woman who brought a mighty Roman general to his ruin—to name a few.

But the playwright's most memorable female lead is, unequivocally, Lady Macbeth.

In significant ways, she is the doppelganger to *Coven*'s key characters; her strength of resolve makes a mockery of her fickle-hearted husband, and the pending Scottish Queen eschews the virtues of motherhood so that nothing may impede her "vaulting ambition."

At first glance, a feminist forebear—and argued to be a witch, too (if only in her temporary allegiance to demonic forces), there is another crucial connection the Lady shares with the Coven: her problematic bi-nature.

In the play's famous "Unsex me here" speech, the co-conspirator to nascent potentate Macbeth perceives that the quickest way to the crown relies upon an extreme measure: excising her womanly nature—

> [Come to my woman's breasts,
> And take my milk for gall, you murdering ministers . . . (*Macbeth*, Act I, Scene v)

> I would, while it was smiling in my face,
> Have pluck'd my nipple from his boneless gums,
> And dash'd the brains out, had I so sworn as you . . . (Act I, Scene vii)

Caroline Cakebread interprets the shocking soliloquy as Lady Macbeth "trading her traditional feminine role as mother and nurturer in exchange for a power which accords with the violent, masculine world of which her husband is a part."

In a Machiavellian tragedy, evil gets you everywhere—for a time—and the aspiring mistress of misrule determines that to achieve her ends, her diabolical side must become her sum total.

Shades of the doomed Queen and her disdain for her "sentimentalized" sex are made manifest in *Coven*—unmistakably so in Delphine's gleeful recount of her exsanguinating her husband's bastard baby ("*Coven*: The Dead"); Marie Laveau's annual child sacrifice to Papa Legba in exchange for immortality ("*Coven*: The Magical Delights of Stevie Nicks"); and Fiona slitting the throat of her charge, Madison ("*Coven*: The Replacements"). In defying their maternal nature—"unsexing" themselves—the women take their place in the void beyond salvation, damned.

Lady Macbeth's attempt to deny the gentler part of herself—so that she may do her bloody work unfettered—is shown to be futile; the light and dark of her person are inexorably enmeshed, and she ultimately reveals herself to be "good," too—in that she has a conscience—strong enough to plunge her into guilt-ridden madness.

Watch Her Burn

Rock on, ancient queen
Follow those who pale in your shadow.

—Fleetwood Mac, "Gold Dust Woman"

The desert shimmers beneath her sanguineous, billowing gown; eyes inscrutable, painted black. Attended upon to her death like a Tudor queen, she takes her place at the stake in splendor—hands bound, yet unassailably regal. Then flames enfold her and the witch ignites in a blaze of pyretic magnificence. Her last word—an ode to her couturier god—carried on the wind, even as nothing of Myrtle Snow remains but the crimson ash of her regalia swirling heavenward.

Coven's finale brings the raging against forces within and without full circle: a witch must burn.

There is no place for wholly happy endings in a show like *American Horror Story*; whether or not "good" prevails, there's always the ironic aside—an homage to life's paradox: for good to win, there must be an evil to conquer.

Zoe is a character defined by this irony; a parodic juxtaposition of bad luck and serendipity (or destiny) —although the seeming antipodes appear to fit, as if fate has interceded with a burlesque sense of humor. Her sweetheart Kyle may be dead, but his already-necrotic boy parts are the perfect partner to her killer vagina; *and so*, Zoe has found true love (albeit with a Frankensteinian creation). This is, perhaps, the teen witch's most telling "contradiction": she gets her fairy tale. Because, while she may be a budding feminist in everything but name, she's also *still just a girl.*

Though she lives through to the credit roll, Zoe doesn't end up being *the* heroine. The girl in the summer of her youth, with powers censured by immense responsibility, is still learning the art of compromise without entirely capitulating to either of her natures: witch, or woman.

Social historian Martha Rampton describes the current breed of feminism as an expression of ambiguity; the celebration of femininity alongside a view towards gender equality. If Zoe and the metaphor of her growing pains embodies the hope of this modern feminism—Myrtle Snow is its full realization.

Unlike Zoe, Myrtle is entirely complicit in the expression of her duality. She may be the "baddest witch," Fiona's nemesis, but in terms of virtue, she is not the villainous Supreme's diametric opposite. A double-edged character, her depiction as a righteous Christ is unmistakeable in the Biblical allusions—wrongly accused ("*Coven*: Burn, Witch. Burn!"), resurrected from the dead ("*Coven*: The Sacred Taking"), and in *Coven*'s most unsubtle allegory, as head of the table in a *Last Supper*-before-Seven-Wonders tableau ("*Coven*: The Seven Wonders"); she also possesses a cunning craftiness that typifies her as the 'traditional' witch—shameless chicanery

("*Coven*: The Sacred Taking") and eye-gouging *à la* melon baller ("*Coven*: Head") are not beneath her. But Myrtle is all about context; her malfeasance is primarily purposed for ousting Fiona and protecting the Coven, and even with this justifiability, she insists upon adhering to the letter of the law and paying for her crimes.

The Head of the Witches' Council is an especially poignant contrast to her peers because she *embraces* her plural natures; she is at once a witch to be reckoned with, a hopeless romantic who lives vicariously through Zoe and Kyle's relationship, and throughout, an enduring stand-in mother for Cordelia. (*And* she does it all in *haute couture*.)

She's no Lady Macbeth—she accepts what she is in totality, and uses it.

She is also "Guardian of Veracity," gifted with a potent talent for truth spells, but most prominently, an incisive intuition; it is this quest for *truth,* not a decorous aspiration to be "good," which acts as her governing force. And she is successful in her methods—the Coven is saved, and a new generation of witches lives to take a stand against the darker shadows in the shifting moral grey.

Myrtle, then, is the working antithesis to the flaws of Natural Law's routine application. She is an empowered amalgam of dissonant identities, unbound by the inconstant constellation of what is "good" or "evil," instead using her intuitive sense and determination for truth as lodestar. To quote Kyle Cupp's postmodern revision, Natural Law shouldn't be "a laundry list of moral norms covering every possible situation and circumstance. It's a guide to the discernment that each person has to make in her unique time and place." Amorphous morality be damned—even when Myrtle insists upon her own execution ("*Coven*: The Seven Wonders"), it's not to bring quasi-rectitude to the Coven, but practically, to exorcise the re-branded academy of its remaining link to the past.

"I go proudly to the flame," the defender of truth proclaims ("*Coven*: Burn, Witch. Burn!"). This is but the *first* of her burnings—like accused witch Joan of Arc, she is punished at the pyre more than once. In totality, Myrtle's life and death (*both* of them) invoke a breathtaking, scorchingly beautiful portrait of that sainted kindred spirit; the peasant girl turned heroine of France, whose own legacy of martyrdom reiterates: It's no easy path for the agent of change. *Discord is inevitable*.

Confronted with the stunning image that is the martyr-witch, Natural Law falls short as a tablet of commandments. Its usefulness instead is that in *Coven*'s metaphors deconstructing its precepts as absolutes, the theory succinctly encapsulates the ambiguity of the feminist experience. Natural Law consequently describes women as we are, *by design*: diverse, conflicted, straining under and striving through a weight of incoherent longings. This is our nature. And to fight for truth is to kindle our inborn antagonism.

Aquinas believed that we could never actually attain complete happiness in this life. Our time on Earth is intended for strife, the perpetual struggle towards resolution; transcendent peace. Thus, for the feminist, there never was and never will be a full realization of her purpose.

Her nature precludes it. She was born to burn.

IV

I am tough, but I'm no cookie

14
The Absurdity at the Heart of Horror

GERALD BROWNING

Like a monstrous salivating beast, absurdity jumps out at you from every episode of *American Horror Story*.

American Horror Story uses a similar ensemble cast to tell different tales of the macabre each season. Each story is told in a different time, with mostly different characters. Each with different horrific tones. All of these stories have a similar unsettling feeling, but one concept that is readily apparent in this series, as well as in most horror movies, is absurdity.

We often call something "absurd" if it's simply ridiculous. Philosophically, however, the word conveys something a bit different. In Albert Camus's *The Myth of Sisyphus*, the term "absurdity" describes the human condition—the quest to find meaning in a meaningless universe.

Sisyphus, the literary symbol of absurdity, was a king who was punished by the gods for his deceitful nature. He was condemned to eternally push a boulder up a hill, only to have it inevitably roll back down. This punishment forces him to face the futility of his existence.

Sisyphus's plight is a mirror on the human condition. Our attempts to find meaning in our existence are confounded by the meaninglessness of our circumstances. *American Horror Story* illustrates, in stark and realistic fashion, that true horror is found in the meaninglessness of life. The angels, demons, vampires, ghosts, zombies, and other creatures of the macabre, act as a metaphor for just how senseless life is.

Absurdity and Horror

Absurdity and horror stories are often paired. One of the most powerful story devices used in horror (especially in horror movies) is the notion that the end returns to the beginning. Horror characters confront the absurd when they inevitably realize that they have gone through terrible, gruesome experiences, all for nothing. The villain (monster, demon, or demented serial killer) will return to what he or she has been doing since the story began. This creates a situation of infinite and continuous horror. Season Two of *American Horror Story* hints at this. In *Asylum*, the song "Dominique" was played continuously throughout the season. This song became a cue, strategically placed to contrast a horrible or violent scene with the serene song (which ended up creating an eerie mood).

Another major theme in horror stories that highlights absurdity and meaninglessness is immortality. What is life worth to supernatural or paranormal creatures who can outlive the normal human being? Would an infinitely long life entail infinite absurdity? In Season Five, the Countess (played by Lady Gaga), a vampire, sees little value in life and consequently retreats to a hedonistic (almost libertine) way of "living." She collects lovers, and discards them in much the same way that we would discard a worn pair of shoes.

In Season One, we don't encounter vampires, but there are ghosts. In the universe of *Murder House*, ghosts cannot really engage with the living outside of the house that they are haunting (except on Halloween). In this season, the Harmons, a troubled family, move into an old Hollywood house that is haunted by the many spirits who have been murdered there. The longer the family stays in the house, the more dangerous it becomes. Eventually, the house kills them all and they are doomed to remain there for eternity. Ironically, the Harmons are not truly happy until they are reunited as ghosts.

There's absurdity in the fact that each dead member of the family tries to protect the other, living members. The endeavor is pointless—the writing is on the wall. Once the Murder House has its sights on someone, there's no getting out alive. Like Sisyphus with his rock, the naive owners of the Murder House engage in a futile struggle to impose order on chaos.

Another existential phenomenon that puts us face-to-face with the absurd is our attempt to understand and characterize the world around us. Though humans have made miraculous advances in science, there is still much that we don't understand. What's more, even if we grant that the human species has made remarkable progress in understanding the external world, any individual human only possesses some small subset of that knowledge. We die too soon to truly reach knowledge of a critical mass.

This lack of understanding contributes to a sense of insignificance and existential despair. Sometimes the only response to that despair is to embrace our own insignificance. Camus illustrates this point in a poignant passage from *The Myth of Sysiphus*:

> And here are trees and I know their gnarled surface, water and I feel its taste. These scents of grass and stars at night, certain evenings when the heart relaxes—how shall I negate this world whose power and strength I feel? Yet all the knowledge in the world will not convince me that this world is mine. You describe it to me and you teach me to classify it. You enumerate its laws and in my thirst for knowledge I admit that they are true. You take apart its mechanism and my hope increases. At the final stage you teach me that this wondrous and multicolored universe can be reduced to the atom and that the atom itself can be reduced to the electron. All this is good and I wait for you to continue. But you tell me of an invisible planetary system in which electrons gravitate around a nucleus. You explain the world to me with an image. I realize then that you have been reduced to poetry: I will never know. What need had I of so many efforts? The soft lines of these hills and the hand of evening on this troubled heart teach me much more. (pp. 19–20)

Supernatural phenomena play a similar role in *American Horror Story*—forcing the show's characters to look the absurd straight in the face. In each season, it becomes clear pretty quickly that the characters are insignificant and powerless against a wide range of forces that they do not understand. How can they navigate the world around them when they don't fully understand it?

When the Harmons purchased the Murder House, they had no idea what they were getting themselves into. Presumably, they had no experience to speak of with the ghostly realm prior to moving in. As a result, when bizarre things started to take place, they couldn't understand what was happening around them and were not in a position to predict what might be coming next. They couldn't protect themselves because they couldn't comprehend the true nature of the threat.

This theme comes up again in *Asylum*. The Nazi scientist, turned resident physician, Dr. Arthur Arden, attempts to study aliens in Season Two. As an advocate of eugenics, Dr. Arden attempts to exert control over the world by manipulating it. Through his experiments, he hopes to create a master race that would be capable of surviving nuclear fallout. He's entranced when he learns that Kit Walker has truly been abducted by aliens, entities that appear to be far more advanced than human beings in every way. He does everything he can to somehow harvest the power of the alien race. At the end of the day, he isn't able to make any significant progress toward that end because he simply can't understand the phenomenon he is trying to study. Pepper, imbued with a new confidence, understanding, and the newfound ability to speak after her abduction by aliens, returns with a mission from the alien race to protect the now pregnant Grace. When Dr. Arden tries to perform an x-ray to see the life that is growing inside Grace, Pepper refuses to allow him to go through with it. She says:

> Stupid man. You think they'd allow you to continue your barbaric practice? She's protected. Your x-rays won't penetrate her body.

> You'll see nothing. Oh, but they've been watching you. You think you're like them with your clumsy experiments. But they laugh at you Dr. Arden. They make jokes. Here's a good one. Knock knock. Who's there? Arden? Arden who? Arden you quack who would make a better duck?

The universe plays the role for us that the aliens play in Dr. Arden's story. Dr. Arden builds a sadistic career out of an attempt to understand the world so that he can manipulate it to his advantage. In the end, it crystal clear exactly how futile and insignificant his progress has really been. Similarly, no matter how much effort we exert toward understanding the complexity of the universe, true comprehension will always be beyond our grasp. Perhaps we, too, would make better ducks.

The theme is carried through into *Coven.* Zoe believes herself to be an ordinary, run-of-the-mill young lady. Her world is shattered when she realizes that she has the "power" to kill those who have intercourse with her. This realization initiates her awakening. She is reborn as a witch. She is now forced to try to understand and navigate a world that is unlike anything she has ever known. The witchcraft is just beginning. There are forces, such as the forces of the undead, which seem to defy all explanation.

These same barriers to understanding come up again and again in the other seasons in the series. In Season Four, *Freak Show,* the supernatural comes in the form of ghosts like Edward Mordrake, who haunt the freaks on Halloween to hear the horrible stories that the sideshow performers have to tell. In Season Five, *Hotel*, the Hotel Cortez is haunted by spirits and vampires. Ghosts also haunt the cast of *Roanoke*. In each season, the rules that govern the supernatural realm are different and are difficult or impossible for the characters to apprehend. Again, the attempt to understand is futile.

Just when we seem to understand the world, it changes. Sometimes we encounter the absurd when we recognize the impermanence of the things we care about. Throughout the series, when humans interact with the supernatural, they are rocked with existential shock. They realize that what they once thought was real is real no longer, if it was ever real to begin with. How does one feel when the world, as they know it, is no more? Monsters are real. The illusions of safety and comfort are shattered.

When we watch a horror movie or a television series such as *American Horror Story*, we see characters fighting for survival. Season Six is filmed in an often-used example of postmodern horror storytelling: found footage. With this method, we are able to see the raw fear of the characters as they scramble to survive the night, when the dead come for them. The interesting aspect of horror stories is the fact that we know (because of the genre of the story) that the characters' lives are forfeit and they are prolonging the inevitable. As a viewer, one may wonder why they would fight so hard to live when their demise is inevitable. Much like Sisyphus, futilely pushing the boulder up the hill, these characters desperately cling to their lives. They go through horrific task after task to survive the night. However, we're aware that the lives of the actors of *My Roanoke Nightmare* would not survive the night.

Horror and Nihilism

It's hard to miss the nihilistic elements of *American Horror Story*. In the Marquis de Sade's work, titled *Justine*, we see the horrors visited upon the titular character by libertines who believe in no God or anything save the pleasure that they wish to receive from committing acts of horror. In *American Horror Story*, we see similar nihilistic sensibilities in some of the characters. Characters such as *Murder House's* Tate Langdon exhibit nihilistic tendencies, as evidenced by the fact that he saw no purpose in life and decided to shoot up his school. The Countess embraces a hedonistic worldview. Paradoxically, death seems to deprive life of meaning and to confer meaning on life. Does eternal life entail an eternity of absurdity? The Countess seems to think so, and to cover up the void that she feels, she decides to create children who are also vampiric immortals to spend eternity with her.

In *Murder House,* Mrs. Harmon's baby is very important to those that live and haunt the House. The baby, a creation of human and ghost, represents the end of the world. Babies are often use as symbols of innocence. Casting such a creature as the ultimate evil is an absurd juxtaposition. The recognition of absurdity is, in many ways, the destruction of innocence.

In addition to the case of the *Murder House* baby, we see innocence destroyed in other seasons as well. In *Freak Show*, one of Elsa Mars's dearest "attractions" is Ma Petite. Everyone in the freak show loves her. Her sweet, innocent persona highlights the depravity of another character—Dell Toledo. Dell is a carnival strongman who is also a closeted homosexual. His uber-masculine persona is overcompensation for the self-loathing he feels for his inability to come to terms with who he is. His secret is discovered by the opportunistic conman named Stanley, who seduces Toledo and later blackmails him into killing one of the "freaks" so that Stanley can sell the corpse to a museum. Stanley wants the hands of Jimmy Darling. Dell refuses to comply because Jimmy is Dell's own son. Instead, he selects Ma Petite. She is murdered.

The world of *Freak Show*, and the world of *American Horror Story* in general, is exceptionally dark. Ma Petite is a light in the darkness. The desire to preserve that light is a desire that the universe doesn't care to accommodate. The universe is not the kind of thing that can care. As Camus says, absurdity consists in a confrontation between the desires of the individual and an indifferent universe. We want Ma Petite's light to go own shining brightly, but it's easily snuffed out.

The End

American Horror Story highlights our more basic Human Horror Story. It shows us the true horror of life—its meaninglessness. We encounter absurdity when we seek meaning in a meaningless universe. Mankind has always wondered, "Why do bad things happen to good people?" The true horror is the answer: because they do. There's nothing more to the answer than that. The nihilistic elements that we see in horror stories act as a reaction to mankind's constant need to find meaning in life.

We want to be here for a purpose, a legitimate reason. The absurdity that we see in *American Horror Story* comes down to one irrefutable truth: there is no reason.

15
Red Harvest in Roanoke

FERNANDO GABRIEL PAGNONI BERNS AND EMILIANO AGUILAR

In Chapter 8 of *American Horror Story's* Season Six ("Roanoke"), one character belonging to a TV show's crew explains to her companions (and by extension, to us, friendly viewers) that the full moon is "female energy." She further adds, "Mother Moon affects everything, from the tides to fertility and the menstrual cycle."

In the episode, she is depicted as a shallow attention-seeker who only wants to go viral on the Internet by recording supernatural shenanigans. Hollow as she is, however, what she says is true. Part of "Roanoke" is inextricably attached to femininity, motherhood, and the gifts that Mother Nature gives to humanity.

Roanoke is about a TV crew documenting what occurs within haunted woods populated by evil pig-men and a female Butcher who hunts pesky humans through the wilderness. This particular season of *American Horror Story* is a perfect case study from the perspective of ecocriticism.

What is ecocriticism? It's a new discipline which analyzes cultural texts from an ecological perspective. Ecocritics tie their cultural analyses explicitly to a Green program. Ecocriticism is closely related to environmentally oriented developments in philosophy such as advances in animal rights or studies of the depiction of natural landscapes in fiction. Ecocriticism investigates the relationship between human beings and human production (culture) and the non-human world (Nature) fiction or film.

Historically, culture and nature are classified as opposites—as "enemies." Culture is what differentiates us from animals and nature in general. The concept of culture is not separable from the human domination of nature. Prosperity is achieved thanks to the domination of nature through the growth of human technology and science.

Urbanites and Rednecks

The series begins with a marked culture-Nature divide: it tells the story of the Millers (Shelby and Matt), a couple who have suffered a brutal assault which left Matt temporarily hospitalized and caused Shelby to have a miscarriage (they were attacked after watching the feature film *Red Harvest* in a theater, an ironic signpost of what lies ahead of them. Red harvests, indeed!).

They decide to leave the unsafe city to live in a large house in the North Carolina woods. The story of nature as a place of exile to which urbanites flee, however, is enhanced by the presence of media: in fact, viewers are watching not the real thing, but a series of dramatizations made for a show called *My Roanoke Nightmare*. This is the main scenario in which Nature (the forests) battles with Culture (the city and media).

After moving in, the Millers perceive nature in two predominant ways: first, as a sanitized thing. Both wife and husband walk aimlessly through the forest, enjoying Mother Nature, with singing birds as a backdrop. They even carry a lunch box, invoking the image of a bucolic picnic. But don't forget the *Horror* in *American Horror Story*—soon enough, Nature starts to show its ugly face. And it is ugly indeed.

Shortly after they move in, weird phenomena start to occur. They hear the squeal of pigs through the night, and some kind of big creature seems to be on the loose around the house, causing havoc. Shelby is attacked in her bathtub by ghostly inhabitants of the forests and skinned pigs are left in front of the Millers' house. Little Blair Witch–like totems made with weeds are left in the house after a particular nasty assault. Everything related to the forest or animals seems to be against them. In one scene in Chapter One, the entire forest unnaturally moves around Shelby. To make things worse, a rain of teeth falls hard upon the house.

Roanoke questions the idea that nature has been dominated by the Age of Reason. The power of Nature is still there. The show-within-the-show even uses the sketch of a tree with bloody roots as logo. As horror, *Roanoke* deliberately takes the fears provoked by the dualistic separation of humans from nature promoted by Western philosophy and makes them the cause for horror.

The Butcher, one of the main villains of *Roanoke*, continues to exist because of the bond she shares with the land that she protects from invaders. Supposedly, after the sacrifices given to Earth, the land opens up to drink the sacrificial blood and gives, in return, better future harvests. Birth (the fertility of the Earth) is paid with death (sacrifice). This cycle of harvest is connected with menstrual blood and human pregnancy, so dangerous Nature is associated with femininity. The power of the forest is potentiated by Matt's sexual act with the Witch of the Wood, creating a bond that ensures that the Millers will not be able to escape from Roanoke (they come back in the second season of the show-within-the-show).

Mother Nature Is Bad-Tempered

Ecocriticism is strongly linked to feminism. *Roanoke*'s approach is, broadly speaking, ecofeminist in inspiration, drawing on what audiences can see as a powerful (and, in this case, sinister) shared commitment on the part of women to the nurture and protection of Mother Earth.

Ecocriticism identifies the dualism of culture and nature as the ultimate source of anti-ecological beliefs and practices, such as deforestation. But a branch of ecocriticism, ecofeminism, also blames the dualism of man and woman.

Patriarchy, the social and cultural discourses that support the supremacy of man and everything "manly" over anything feminine, distinguishes humans from nature on the grounds of some alleged quality such as rationality, and then assumes that this distinction confers superiority upon humans. Patriarchy also distinguishes men from women on the grounds of some alleged quality such as . . . well . . . rationality, and then assumes that this distinction confers superiority on men.

Ecofeminism involves the acknowledgment that these two arguments share a common attitude of domination in which women have been associated with nature (due to irrationality), while men have been associated with culture (intellect, domination of the irrational) and that this should suggest a common struggle between women and nature, both exploited by men. Women and nature are "sisters," united against male domination.

In *Roanoke*, the ecofeminist approach is present from the start, provocatively subverting the conventional philosophical approaches by identifying the patriarchal assumptions at work sustaining our vision of nature as completely dominated by humans. The ideal of a dominated nature is determined by the demands of technology sustained, in turn, by the scientific mind (male rationalism). *Roanoke* playfully undermines the assumption of both nature and women as completely dominated and integrated into the patriarchal mindset. Instead, Nature and women are aligned together as powerful beings with agency of their own.

While Matt states that he feels "at home" in their new house, Shelby—more attuned to her natural surroundings—claims to have perceived some sense of menace around her ("From the very first moment I felt . . . danger there"). This suggests that she's closer to Nature, while Matt, as a man (more related to culture), is easily deceived by a bucolic surface.

Who is the one traveling to the city for work and who is the person staying in the house? Right. *He* is the one who keeps coming and going, while *she* must remain in the house, thus linking natural and supernatural phenomena (like a rain of teeth) to her. Matt does not even believe his wife after she explains to him that teeth were falling from the sky. Feverish imagination and female imagination have been deemed as irrational acts that are related to feminine logic, or lack of thereof.

Since Nature is irrational, there is a clear bond between women and Nature. Shelby's "ecological" warnings are downplayed as irrational things when, in fact, she would have saved everyone if somebody had listened to her.

The nature-centric approach of ecofeminism sees the domination of Nature, and its instrumental status as a resource to be used and exploited, as deeply linked to the male exploitation of women. Matt works in the pharmaceutical industry, an industry based on the exploitation of natural resources. Shelby, by contrast, is a yoga teacher and practitioner, furthering the relationship of her with the environment.

Yoga is a discipline that stimulates spiritual states and inner peace while proposing a more natural way of life. The word yoga derives from the Sanskrit root *yuj*, which means to connect, so this discipline cannot but be ecological-oriented as it proposes healthier links with the environment. Shelby is also allergic to gluten, thus furthering her "fragile" persona, which makes her akin to the vulnerability of nature, always on the brink of extinction. Lee, Matt's sister, even mocks Shelby's "bland" personality.

Lee seems to be co-opted by patriarchy. Lee is a tough ex-cop who loves guns and despises "feminine" things (like yoga, which is not even a job!). She likes the city and finds the wilderness surrounding the house mostly uninteresting. Lee, a hard-as-nails woman, subverts the essentialized notion of women as fragile things. In fact, she is an equal to her husband, also a cop. She is also a mother—much of the narrative of *Roanoke* revolves around Lee's attempts to get custody of her only daughter, Flora (you'll have spotted the nature-related name). Lee and Shelby cannot be more different. However, both will have a close relationship with Nature, thus downplaying any stereotypical conception about the relationship between women and the non-human world.

The metaphor of "Mother Nature" is crafted within a patriarchal ideology that justifies the "natural" role of women: motherhood and submissiveness. Further, the lunar cycles and the seasonal times of agriculture mirror the menstrual sequence, so womanhood is inextricably linked, for better or worse, to Earth and Nature.

With this in mind, it's easy to see why motherhood is important in *Roanoke*. Lee herself explains that there is a "special bond" between mother and daughter. In fact, Lee will act as a force of Nature, eliminating everything that stands in her way to win custody of her daughter. Toward this end, she kills her ex-husband in the forest, with the help of some complicity from the woods.

The Butcher and the mother of the Polk family are also important matriarchal figures. Mama Polk answers to the Butcher, and she is another woman who privileges motherhood. She is a cold-blood killer, who tortures Lee and Audrey while slowly eating her human victims, but she is first and foremost, a mother, another woman who is unstoppable once her sons are in danger or killed.

All these women are modeled after the main mother of the story: the Butcher. The creation of the female Butcher is related to a great hunger that took place in the sixteenth century, when the land did not provide enough to keep the people well fed.

Thomasin's back story is constructed around stereotypes on gender. Thomasin was married to the governor of the Roanoke colony (seemingly, populated mostly by men), assaulted by a huge hunger. Men want meaty meals and Thomasin cannot provide anything but vegetables. The colony rebels and when Thomasin's husband was gone, a group of men took the woman out into the woods and left her to starve to death. There, she makes a deal with a personification of the forest and the matriarch is later turned into the bloodthirsty Butcher, a ghost whose main mission is to keep the land soaked in blood and, in doing so, greener and richer in vegetation.

Thomasin and Nature, both previously brutally exploited by the colony, now rise to dominate Roanoke though supernatural powers. It is the complicated relationship of men with the environment which gives birth to the female Butcher rather than any evilness inherent in women.

According to the traditional view, Nature is useless if not integrated into the social. Representing nature as threatening has been, historically, a good tool to promote submission. Nature becomes a good thing only as a result of human intervention. People constructed this narrative to justify human actions such as deforestation, pollution, and devastation of natural resources. In popular culture, hostile nature is eventually mastered through male heroism, technology and the killing or taming of animals. In the horror genre, this idea is often subverted: Nature fights back and can turn the tables on human exploitation.

The idea of wilderness, signifying nature in a state uncontaminated by civilization, is a potent construction of nature, and is found in both the philosophy of ecology and in *Roanoke*. The series plays with the images of nature as savage and evil, with humans trying to "tame" wilderness through media. But as a horror show, *Roanoke* has "permission" to show humans failing miserably in their doomed attempts to control and exploit the wilderness, here, a real menace.

Cutting Animals

The depiction of animals in media, within the philosophy of ecocriticism, has become a central emblem for an ecological awareness.

The Millers' first clash with Nature takes place before they actually move in: when buying the house, the Millers have to interact with the Polks, a family of rednecks who, clearly, are not enthusiastic about the couple from Los Angeles settling in. As even a casual viewer of horror film and TV knows—and we can assume that any viewer of American Horror Story is more than "casual"—rednecks are always bad news: they are figures born from the savage and bestial wilderness, animal-like rather than entirely human. The Polks are a slightly more "human" version of the deadly and ghostly pig-men that the couple will face later in the show.

In horror fiction, rednecks are depicted as closer to the animal sphere thanks to their animal-like existence on the economic and physical fringes of society and culture, thus presenting an interesting topic of investigation for ecocriticism: if the human sphere and the non-human sphere were conceptualized as sharing nothing in common, then the presence of animal-like people is a form of hybridism or impurity. This hybridism will increase after the pig-men show up. Rednecks are usually depicted in film as at least slightly deformed, thus enhancing their link with animals. The rednecks scaring the Millers, indeed, have some deformities: one of them has animal-like teeth pushing out of his mouth, making the owner look bestial.

The Butcher, meanwhile, is the one in charge of animalizing people. After all, she is a butcher, a person in charge of killing and cutting animals into pieces. In *Roanoke*, this particular butcher prefers to cut human beings into pieces. Even so, she animalizes her victims first. Animalizing, a kind of metaphor, is central to the contemporary ecological movement. It involves giving an animal texture to human beings—giving animal properties to people.

At the beginning of Chapter Two, the butcher is killing a male victim. She calls him a "clawed beast" who rots in the mud and filth. The Butcher's acolytes fit a pig head onto the man's head and then proceed to roast him in fire, as an animal. The Butcher has killed a man, but she first animalized him.

Animalizing is important to ecocriticism because it intertwines the animal with the human, producing a hybrid, something that does not easily fit into a category. Hybridism ruptures the idea of the spheres of the human and the animal as mutually exclusive, privileging rather the notion sustained by many within ecocriticism that humans are just another kind of animal, no more and no less. That is why ecocriticism privileges the term "non-human animal" to describe what most people simply call "animals."

The idea of humans as another kind of animal severely disturbs the hierarchy that positioned humans above animals, a hierarchy that promotes exploitation. This can be observed in the way in which the Polks treat their children—like animals. They live within a barn, eating with their hands—pure filth and bestial behavior. They are animal-like, humans behaving like beasts, indicating that civility is something that is produced—a social construction rather than some "essential" condition of humans. If not properly attended, people could "descend" to the level of animals. People are always on the brink of becoming animals. It is just a small step.

The menacing presence of the pig-men is another display of hybridism since they are half humans and half pigs. Contradictorily, the pig-men hunt humans, thus furthering the idea of human beings as just another form of animal and cleverly subverting the rigid hierarchies that postulate animals as objects to be hunted.

(Non) Cute Animal Videos

The last years have brought about changes in the way people address environmental issues in America: TV broadcasts ecological documentaries and cute videos with animals 24/7, including shocking scenes of animals attacking other animals (and people) or ecological deterioration. As nature is destroyed by humans, people are hungry for virtual images of untamed Nature. In this sense, "Return to Roanoke" provides both, images of ghosts and nature, both equally eerie.

The omnipresence of social networks is foreshadowed from day one in "Return to Roanoke." In the confessional installed in the mansion, Dominic recognizes that the most important thing for him is screen time. Fans of the show walk through the woods, unaware of the marvelous and dangerous Nature surrounding them. They are thrilled about the idea of their popularity increasing on the web, making exclamations like, "How many likes you think we'll get on Instagram?" or "We are gonna blowup the Internet!" Nature is mostly invisible for them, just a necessary creepy backdrop for their little tales of ghosts.

The strength of the images of the diverse characters fighting the horrors of Nature is so powerful that a fan of *My Roanoke Nightmare* states that "Roanoke is the only thing that kept me going," giving to the show an overwhelming power. People seem connected to technology, as cyborgs, the same way that the people within the woods are connected to animals, both turned hybrid.

Since the show revolves around media and technology, the culture-nature contrast is more pronounced. Those within the house use technology as a way of capturing nature: cell phones, television, VHS, and digital media are used as a way to dominate the landscapes around them. They want to capture Nature as a way to control it.

Media technology is associated with the consumption of natural resources used to manufacture screens and hardware. The development of technology constitutes a shift from a nature-centered way of life to a technology-centered one, in which the latter has the power to reconstruct images of ecology to fit the interest of viewers. Here, producers try to re-configure nature as scary and sell it that way to audiences. Woods are transformed into rating figures, while people see grisly wilderness from the safety of their homes. The power of Nature, however, will resurface with creepy new powers to destroy those trying to tame the woods.

The fake ghosts and creepiness of the woods become real. People do not leave nature alone, so Nature strikes back. Nature collides with the alienation provoked by the media and people start to mistake fiction for reality, made-up characters for the real things.

The most obvious and pathetic example is Agnes, the actress who plays the Butcher in the documentary: she reflects the duality of the urbanite as a victim but at the same time, a victimizer. Although her actions are product of a mental disturbance (satirizing actors who seek to "get deeply involved" in a particular role), that disturbance takes her to the woods to continue killing in the name of something previously "scripted."

In the woods, in Nature, she seems to have found something real in a world of artifice. Her own bloody death. Nature, in the end, has won.

16
Please Don't Kill Me! (But if You Do, Could You Make a Video?)

CHERISE HUNTINGFORD

"*Croatoan* . . . ," it whispers.

Can you feel that cold finger on the periphery of your consciousness? The one tracing its subtle tattoo of unease—a superstitious, creeping dread of some faceless, even amorphous, threat?

It's a celluloid cliché, sure, but it's those plentiful, unforgettable, horror stories that have taught us to respond as such; the familiar incantation summoning an unknown denizen of dark places, or uttered like a hex to send hell-beasts screaming back to the Pit.

In real life, Croatoan's associations possess the gravitas of something perhaps more terrifying. Historically, the name lays claim to that ill-fated, infamous Lost Colony of Roanoke, where 115 English settlers, whether by mutiny, xenophobic savagery, or—the more popular retelling—by a less discernible agent swathed in supernatural overtones, disappeared from the New World island without a trace.

For now, the vanishing en masse has its historicity hidden by the narrative form of legend; in *whatever* retelling, however, it's that "*without a trace*" bit that really gets us— the non-mythologised missing piece that sets the fear-driven lizard brain into overdrive and pushes our higher powers of comprehension to the brink of combustion. How can you just . . . *disappear*? With nothing left behind to tell your real story? (Or at least a version of your own authorship?)

The chances of falling victim to the anonymous forces that conspired in the sixteenth-century Americas may be slim, but the struggle to grasp the finality of corporeal existence, and the gnawing disquiet over the potential nothingness thereafter, is endemic to the human condition—because it is our universal fate.

Sans sentiment or compunction, *American Horror Story: Roanoke* eviscerates this meticulously repressed fear and sticks it on a pyke. (Screw psychotherapy.)

What *remains* is a remains-splattered smorgasbord of ritual sacrifice, hedonistic torture, cannibalism, matricide, senicide, and familicide—and the confrontation with the blood, bone, and gristle of our own mortality.

We can, of course, just flip the channel. Yet the knowledge will still be there; even as canned laughter drowns out that whisper, or as Rachael Ray effuses nirvanic joy whilst stuffing a turducken—it's there, insidiously lurking off-camera.

So we remain fixed to the screen as the Butcher disembowels an innocent victim like she's unwinding a garden hose, indulging a sadomasochistic agony over how we go on *living* knowing that we, too, are only a few scene changes away from the final fade-out.

How *do* we deal, then?

Come—chew on a bit of Mama Polk's special jerky, as we ruminate this less palatable predicament of our humanness . . .

It's the Blood Moon, There's Got to be Some Mumbo-Jumbo We Can Use!

Trespassers beware: whatever the Butcher leaves breathing, the shape-shifting Reaper will helpfully finish off (in equally inventive ways)—if a lucky straggler should happen to live long enough to heed this caveat, however, you'll still be forgiven for thinking dying is pretty much the point of *Roanoke*.

Creative carnage certainly propels plenty of action in the sixth installment of *American Horror Story*, but death, to borrow from that saccharine poeticism, *is not the end*. At least that's what we—and the characters of corpse-party *Roanoke*— tell ourselves to survive another night.

Philosopher Stephen Cave explains that as natural beings operating on an unprecedented level of self-awareness, our "overblown intellectual faculties" tell us that death is both certain—and impossible. Just like the Roanokean mystery, we can't wrap our heads around our own sudden ceasing to be, and, in the context of *American Horror Story*, the idea of imminent death ignites amongst its players an extravagant (scared-shitless) stupefaction.

This tortuously unsolvable conundrum, which Cave coins the "Mortality Paradox," and to assuage its dissonant effects on the psyche, cultural anthropologist Ernest Becker suggests that we search for ways in which to symbolically "cheat" death; to achieve immortality—by whatever definition.

Becker fleshes out his theory in the philosophical and psychoanalytical tour de force *The Denial of Death*, which asserts that human cultures have arisen predominantly out of people's attempts to transcend finite existence through a creation and attachment of symbolic meaning to almost every aspect of life (*every* aspect if you consider Freud even managed to eke something subliminal from being constipated).

Civilization, then, is little more than a product of an elaborate "survival" defense mechanism; our long-standing traditions, our sacred rites—right down do the very banal of our daily rituals exercised in presumption of a certain tomorrow—all are the defiant denial of a certain *end*.

It's Real! Everybody Is Dead!

At first, *Roanoke* doesn't seem to have any other layer apart from the superficial one steeped in gratuitous gore; and of course, part of the plot unfolds before the lens of pseudo-reality TV cameras—the apotheosis of facile, pumped direct from the entertainment effluent pipeline. Yet it's that same sanguine-soaked, tongue-in-cheek conceit of a reality show which hints at a much meatier motif, pulsing just beneath the ripped and rended skin of *Roanoke*'s characters.

Despite even the most amateur of dilettantes lambasting its absence of virtue, the reviled reality oeuvre has a point to make. Back in the swinging Sixties and free-loving Seventies, exploitation cinema was just as criticized for its purposeless immorality—but incognito in darkened movie theaters, filmgoers surreptitiously lapped it up (in copious measure), and this implied a subversive, highly significant story all on its own. It wasn't the specifics of *Cannibal Holocaust*'s or *Texas Chainsaw Massacre*'s narratives, it was the shared response those grindhouse gorefests elicited from the audience: a savoring of the adrenaline rush for the ninety-minute running time, then back to home sweet home and a bogeyman-free bed, lulled into slumber by the assurance that peckish tribesmen were stuck in the jungle and fictional Leatherface would never come for them.

Through the medium of horror—the merciless kind that leaves little hope for the protagonists—a fear-of-death catharsis could take place as audience members would enter the darkness of the hypothetical, vicariously experience a degree of life-threatening terror, and then, with a shuddery exhale of relief, switch the lights back on.

Ryan Murphy and Brad Falchuk pay homage to the seminal exploitation flicks—*TCM* Tobe Hooper's raw and uncomfortably visceral, handheld filming style is unmistakeable in the people-eating Polk torture scenes ("Roanoke: Chapter Eight")—though they opt instead for a contemporary way to frame their story: "reality" TV. The result is not, then, an experiment of cause-and-effect with the titillated observer, watching safely as the hackneyed haunted house becomes a slaughterhouse; but rather an already-scripted *commentary*, on what we would do if the credits rolled, and the monster donning the face of death *was still there*.

As with the exploitation genre, there's an irony inherent in reality TV's bad reputation and its simultaneous popularity. Our consumption says something of our own depravity (or the simple "reality" of humanity), and there's an addictive revulsion in watching the (usually degenerate) "actors"—because they function as our proxies.

In the sixth installment of *American Horror Story*, the infamously vanished sixteenth-century Roanoke settlers are resurrected for modern day audiences. First within the framework of a "true-crime" docudrama, and then a reality TV show, these supernatural Lost Colony revenants are put in place to provoke some impressively unhinged reactions by the human "cast mates." The result is an *American Horror Story* superseding its series's antecedents; an exquisitely repugnant setpiece flaunting the very extremities of human behavior (who can wipe clean from memory *that* brain-pulping scene? ("*Roanoke*: Chapter Eight").

The second half of *Roanoke* in particular—the twisted *Survivor*-style episodes—is not just a satiric jibe at the tactics employed to get ratings, but a sardonic reflection of the viewer; the ways in which the various "reality" stars react to their nearing demise is a product of fiction only in that their doom comes primarily in the form of killer ghosts and a flesh-guzzling family seemingly lifted straight from the set of *Deliverance*—these agents of death aside, the core message is that we are interchangeable with those individuals running, raging, and killing, for their lives. If we too had to face-off the relentless threat of expiration, we would do everything the same. We would, apparently, go completely insane.

Do Any of You Not Get What's Going on Here?

Buffered by the mundanities of the everyday, bubble-wrapped in our magical thinking, our looming death is kept at arm's length—but we're nevertheless afforded the proximitous previews; the car crash on your way to work, the friend with the terminal diagnosis, the high- school reunion where those old classmates not fat and flirting with a coronary have already cashed out on shares six feet under.

American Horror Story: Roanoke amplifies the theme of these snippets with the help of some grisly tropes; painting 'em with buckets of red, and inserting a glimpse into an equally unappealing, just-as-grotesque afterlife.

The Butcher, Piggy Man, the Chens, a pair of killer nurses—and certain housemates, too—to name a few; the "Blood Moon" brings forth this myriad of monsters who stalk the Roanokean "site," collectively representing the inevitability of death. The ensuing terror is Cave's Mortality Paradox blown up jumbo size for our viewing displeasure.

And between the jump-scares there's that favored Shakespearean device, *dramatic irony*—a morbid parody of our mind's answer to the Paradox: the obstinate refusal to acknowledge Fate's bloodied cleaver coming down from just behind. Even hotshot Rory's sudden disappearance and pool of still-warm blood is explained away as a stunt, an easy exit for him to make it in some Hollywood movie ("*Roanoke*: Chapter Seven").

Yet—in spite of one 'explainable' departure, it's kinda impossible for the folks to also ignore that someone's barbecuing human sacrifices in the Millers' old front yard ("*Roanoke*: Chapter Three"), and redecorating their dining area with a "MURDER" mural ("*Roanoke*: Chapter Three")—oh—*and* a crazy bitch channeling a psychotic pilgrim, calling herself the Butcher, is holding malfeasant midnight vigils just outside their door ("*Roanoke*: Chapter Four").

With all that going down, *eventually*, mere denial does not suffice. French savant Michel de Montaigne, wrote "Death has us by the scruff of the neck at every moment"—in this, compared with our penchant for sublimating the uncomfortable, *Roanoke*'s unrefined horror is perhaps more accurate when it comes to the pared-down truth of existence—life *is* simply one long massacre, until the last man (or woman) standing has to give up their own ghost (or turn into one, literally—but more on that later). As Cave points out, being thinking creatures, our rationality compels us to respond to the fact of impending death; there comes a point when covering our eyes is not enough to stop us from seeing the monster between our fingers. The psychological threshold between the reality before us and the dream of invincibility will be breached, or broken—through Fate's intervention, or our own acceptance.

The various *Roanoke* characters' confession-booth soliloquies describe their turmoil with having to come to terms with this nightmare; Dominic's tirade in front of an unmanned camera, waxing and waning between futile rage and the misery of realization ("All I wanted is my own show!"), is especially telling; not just in the absurd, desperate excuses for why he cannot die ("I'm supposed to go to Thailand next month!"), but because nobody is watching—or listening—on the other side ("*Roanoke*: Chapter Eight").

The scariest part of death is not the dying part. It's what comes after—or worse; what doesn't. Even if we face up to our advancing earthly terminus, conceiving of the nullity that might await just beyond is almost always too much. We *have* to be more than incidentally sentient hunks of meat—more than an appetizer for the Polk's dinner table, a jar of pickled ears for their Christmas. We *have* to find existential meaning. Or make it.

What's More Important than Screen Time, Huh?

So here we are. At the summit of "Mount Immortality."

The towering mass, whose peaks are hardly discernible in the nebulous ether above, is not a natural phenomenon. It hasn't materialized spontaneously, or evolved over eons as man has constructed his humble life around it—deferential of its inherent power; a dormant volcano. Instead, like the ancient pyramids, the mountain has arisen out of the labors of mortals, and inside its cavernous spaces there is no divine answer to the existential riddle, only the cadavers of those whose long-ago hope is now but a petrified rictus, still waiting to be ferried into Eternity.

As a human construct, the ascent to "immortality"—as defined by both Cave and Becker—is shaped by the subjective and cultural. To ascribe a deep, metaphysical significance to life—and thus 'cheat' death, we engage in purposeful "immortality projects;" the likes of which have, over the course of our species's tenancy on the planet, formed "the foundation of human achievement . . . the wellspring of religion, the muse of philosophy, the architect of our cities, and the impulse behind the arts."

But this is *American Horror Story* after all; so it's safe to say you can forget church and poetry when it comes to the *Roanoke* way of besting death.

In 1986, social psychologists Jeff Greenberg, Tom Pyszczynski, and Sheldon Solomon set out to expand upon Becker's death-denial thesis, resulting in an extensive, surprising, view of all that counts as *causa sui*—or "immortality projects."

Roman Prinz's Terror Management Theory (TMT) posits that to manage the terror wrought by wanting to live but knowing we'll die, we develop culturally-bound worldviews—which imbue our perception of reality with a reason for the universe, which in turn determines the reason for our existence; often spiritual in nature and transcendent. When worldviews *don't* dictate the certainty of a pending paradise (or even some interdimensional, purgatorial waiting room) the cognitive chaos piqued by entertaining the alternative—the end of consciousness—nevertheless demands that we secure our immortality *somehow*. In the absence of divine intercession, the sole way we can overcome the limitation of our physical selves is by focusing on the symbolic.

This manifests through a creation of legacy: amassing an empire, contributing to society, producing a line of progeny, or achieving a feat that will be remembered long after we've plunged into the void.

An iteration of "divine" intervention *does* pop up in *Roanoke*; although becoming a zombie acolyte for the Butcher, ceaselessly roaming an underground labyrinth à la dead loner aristocrat Edward Mott, or eating witch Scathach's proffered boar heart—in exchange for "real" immortality, seems hardly desirable.

Can this be interpreted as a comment on the fear of the posthumous unknown? Maybe. Regardless, the castmates of "Three Days in Hell" readily eschew God's (and *any* transcendental entity's) purported promise of everlasting life—

choosing the *modern-day* religion—Reality TV—and its alternate promise of fame, instead. A perfect vignette illustrating this crass exchange of immortality projects is when superfans of the show-within-the-show ("My Roanoke Nightmare"), Sophie, Todd, and Milo, travel deeper into the wilderness and towards their deaths—their *central* concern is how the experience will bump up their Twitter following. Which it does, no doubt; except they're too dead by that point to revel in the accomplishment ("*Roanoke*: Chapter Eight").

Question: If a person dies in the woods and there's no one there to post it on YouTube, did it really happen?

Other real-life replicas of how we symbolically dam the space between life and a meaningless non-life include the romantic relationship between Matt and Shelby, and the familial bond between Lee and her daughter, Flora.

In these ways, a worldview where humanity itself provides the elixir of immortality translates into a driving concern for preserving the interpersonal connection, and securing social acceptance.

But, while the above examples of defying our innate pointlessness pose no negative threat against others (in fact, the spousal and mother-child relationships could be deemed *aspirational*—even for their own sake)—a "worldview," by definition, does not always confer morality.

Something about Those Woods Made You Lose Control

In several studies, the Terror Management theorists have noted violence as "an extrapolation of a defensive reaction" against death; numerous contexts involving overt or tacit concepts like "winning," "losing," and "victory" function as figurative stand-ins for the greater triumph over our mortal coil. In our subconscious, which does not distinguish between the metaphor of minutiae and grander experience, subjugating the opposition means we are powerful—and, for a fleeting moment, invincible.

This could be the football match turned feral, or the barroom brawl. It could also be killin' and cookin' your next-door neighbors.

In a *New York Times* article delving into the amassed postulated meanings of cannibalism, author and ex-*Natural History Magazine* editor Erik Eckholm writes that the heinous act—when committed with an unambiguous (albeit perverse) ritualism—is often carried out as a way of communicating with the supernatural—or capturing an enemy's power for oneself.

The *Roanoke* anthropophagists make no bones about why they do what they do—and Mama Polk's matter-of-fact account of their gastronomic evolution reveals a symbolism so rich that, in spite of its inelegant rube delivery, would've made cannibal cognoscente Dr. Lecter salivate:

"We found our power and our place. We knew then, the Polks weren't like any other. We were the first family, and we always will be . . . so long as we keep up traditions," ("*Roanoke*: Chapter Eight").

The bloodlusty matriarch describes her "kin" as set apart from mere mortals (or mere meals), *lasting forever*—provided that they continue to cannibalize; an exercise that, nearly eight decades after the bitter austerity of the Great Depression, holds no necessity for survival . . . at least not as far as *starvation* is concerned.

The Polks' worldview depicts The Butcher as the one who wields Death in the Upper Case, and to keep clear of their own material end, the Polks must capitulate to her demands for human sacrifice. At the same time, they must ease the consequent discomfort of fear and suppression. Considering their precariously subordinate position in the food chain, eating people, quite simply, is how they reinstate some temporal semblance of power over *their* eventual, inescapable extinction.

To loosely paraphrase the Polks, the specifics of *how* we find "our power" over death are unimportant. Centuries' worth of 'immortality projects' may have had a hand in civilization and cultural construction (as Becker theorizes) but if history—and *American Horror Story*—is anything to go by, the ascent to immortality can also be littered with corpses.

Further TMT studies discovered that when we're confronted with death—even its suggestion—we are moved to defend our worldviews in extremist ways. World wars, presidential campaigns, religious fundamentalism—real life is run amok with fear-mongered mobs. Cults are another manifestation of how our survival instincts can override sense, and the Butcher's undead entourage of complicitly maniacal colonists is a sublime allegory—better bearing the torch for Death than being burnt at Her pyre, right?

Of course, it'd be remiss not to mention poor ol' Agnes Mary Winstead, who's convinced she is the incarnation of cleaver-toting White. "I'm so sorry, I just wanted to be on TV," is the schizophrenic's catchphrase as she shifts in and out of cognizance of her awful crimes—until she's cleaved in two by the *bona fide* Butcher, that is (*Because I could not stop for Death, She kindly stopped for me).* When Agnes is denied a role reprisal in the sequel to *My Roanoke Nightmare* ("We only want real people this year") she attempts to gut her way through the show's producer and crew to get the screen time ("*Roanoke*: Chapter Seven"). For the wannabe-Butcher, fame is her single shot at significance, eternal remembrance—if heaven *does* exist, there's no seat reserved for her. Better to play it safe and be on TV.

The Butcher Would Get You Eventually

All our times have come
Here but now they're gone
Seasons don't fear the reaper
Nor do the wind, the sun or the rain, we can be like they are.
Come on baby, don't fear the reaper
Baby take my hand, don't fear the reaper.

—Blue Öyster Cult, *Don't Fear (The Reaper)*

Death is our destiny. And the horror genre itself confronts us with this truth; although that's not what we're buying into when we watch. Even with a story that scares you good and proper, there's a lot of *make-believe* that goes into making it something you'd *want* to see.

In the end, horror, for all its subversive commentary, is just fiction. Even "reality" TV is a farce—and that's the point, really: we wouldn't have it any other way.

"We play pretend!" Audrey tearfully exclaims, as Mama Polk brandishes a pair of pliers primed for her torture ("*Roanoke*: Chapter Eight"). The tool *looks* mighty real, though; and Mama ain't buying the actress's spiel about everything being part of some script. Just a show.

Despite (and because of) her repellent ways, the cannibal's dogged ignorance is as authentic and close to the real world as it gets on *Roanoke*. But Audrey is right—invented narrative is how we deal with death; props distract us from our futility, and the promise of a sequel keeps us sticking to the script.

We play pretend.

Ernest Becker believed that human culture is fundamentally contrived: "Each society is a hero system which promises victory over . . . death."

At their core, the things that seem most antagonistic to preserving life, like *Roanoke*'s acts of indulgent violence and miscellaneous rampant lunacy, are ultimately, ironically, revealed to be in pursuit of living forever. Even the brief idyll of "normalcy"—romantic and maternal love—hint at a more self-serving, albeit subconscious, agenda: forging purpose; chasing immortality.

The sixth season of *American Horror Story* itself is a microcosm of life's essential contrivance; the finale sentimentally orchestrated so that in spite of racking up a hefty body count that would justify her own extermination, sole survivor Lee lives on past the grave—cheating death ("*Roanoke*: Chapter Ten"). Becoming immortal. Of course, ghosts aren't *real*, but the viewers—*we*—don't want endings. Creative storytelling can come in handy with that. Even if it makes little sense as part of the bigger plotline.

When "Croatoan" was found carved into a single wooden post—the only sign of there having been a human presence where the Roanokean colony had once existed—theories abounded as to its meaning.

No one has yet found the answer.

In *Roanoke*, medium Cricket Marlowe yells the word when the Butcher materializes during a séance—but we never fully divine its exact power ("*Roanoke*: Chapter Three").

It's possible that a thousand—maybe even a hundred—years from now, our most zealous markings, etched to preserve some iteration of immortality, will be meaningless.

The only thing that will persist is the certainty of death; whether it comes in a ghostly fog, a horde of hungry hillbillies, or on your way home from the multiplex.

You can distract yourself with a multitude of immortality vanity projects, but like the final scene with Lee's spectre and ghost-girl Priscilla walking back to their "home," to commence with some macabre theatre of playing house, the camera zooms out and the Butcher is still there; holding vigil until the time comes ("*Roanoke*: Chapter Ten").

The *least* devilish or demented of the *Roanoke* personalities, Shelby, commits the unthinkable where everyone else is doing everything imaginable to stay alive: she submits to Death.

When her estranged and entranced husband confesses he's fallen for a witch ("*Roanoke*: Chapter Eight"), she understands her investment in a symbolic *forever* is forfeit. And without immortality, there is only death.

The fact that she takes the task into her own hands (and brains her cheating spouse in the process) is irrelevant; what resonates is that a faith in eternity sets us up for naive complacency—in what could be our one chance at life, and perhaps, the *only* way we can ever truly cheat death is to release the chokehold of fear, *and fiction*, and face up to it.

Does this mean we should slit our own throats to achieve freedom from terror, mastery over mortality?

Turns out that *Roanoke* is but one metaphor for the finite human predicament—and resigned suicide or deranged panic are not our only options for response.

When Michel de Montaigne penned that famous line about death holding us "by the scruff of the neck at every moment," he did not mean to imply that our end is imminent—only *inevitable*.

The thinker is credited with another oft-misunderstood quote—cribbed from Cicero—and uses it to title his most stoic essay on the subject of our certain expiration: "to study philosophy is to learn to die."

It's a sentiment that seems as dire and despairing as his earlier rumination on ever-present Death. But the idea of being cognizant of one's finitude is not intended as such. Instead, the search and discovery of our human truth holds us accountable; in so much as we are to live authentically, in the knowledge that the onward march of time towards that impalpable overpass—or precipice—is inexorable.

Montaigne wrote around half a million words over the span of his life, and almost all pulse with a passion and fervor for the ephemeral aspects of our existence. He records the transient mysteries of sleep, sadness, friendship, children, sex—*and death*. By no means lamenting, he says of his mortality: "I want to arrest the swiftness of its passing by the swiftness of my capture, compensating for the speed with which it drains away by the intensity of my enjoyment. The shorter my lease of it, the deeper and fuller I must make it."

Drinking fully from the cup that drains just as surely as his thirst is quenched, Montaigne contemplates mortality as a series of fleeting moments from which to extract every ounce of pleasure—and even life-affirming pain. Difficult feelings will indeed form part of this moment-by-moment, phenomenological appraisal, but to direct them towards some intangible point outside of *now* is an exercise in absurdity—a figment of a fever dream.

As material creatures, our only reality is the immediate experience; history is a fabrication, the future is just a wish, and even the circumstances of our death can only be wildly imagined—a spectacular horror story.

The Butcher will get you—*eventually*—but there's many a clear night before the Blood Moon summons its mistress.

American Haunting Story

RICHARD GREENE

In each of the first six seasons of *American Horror Story* we're presented with a haunted dwelling. The *Murder House* is inhabited by the ghosts of all who died there. The *Asylum* is haunted by Satan himself, as he possesses Sister Mary Eunice. The New Orleans of *Coven* is chock-a-block with the spirits of its past inhabitants, but perhaps most notably among them is the ghost of the evil Axeman who haunts Miss Robichaux's Academy. Elsa Mars's *Freak Show* gets paid a visit from the legendary Edward Mordrake one Halloween. The *Hotel* Cortez, like the *Murder House*, is full of ghosts from its infamous past. And the woods of Roanoke are haunted by the ghosts of the lost colony's original settlers.

American Horror Story wouldn't be a truly *American* horror story if it didn't contain tales of hauntings. Americans love a good haunting story. Each year, countless scores of ghost and horror enthusiasts go on haunted tours (I've been on several myself), and choose to stay in haunted hotels; there certainly is no shortage of purportedly haunted locations. Nearly every state in the Union has a "famous" haunted house or hotel or prison or hospital for the mentally ill, and reports of hauntings are a part of nearly every state's history. Here are some of America's most celebrated haunted locations.

Murder Houses

There are a number of quite famous haunted houses in the United States, but it seems appropriate to begin with the one that served as the inspiration for Season One of *American Horror Story*: the Los Feliz Murder House. This house is reportedly haunted by a physician who in 1959 killed his wife with a ball-peen hammer, attempted to kill his oldest daughter (she escaped to the neighbor's house), and then took his own life. The house has been uninhabited for most of the last fifty-eight years, but was rented briefly for a period just after the murders. The tenants fled the house on the anniversary of the murder-suicide claiming that ghosts were after them.

Perhaps the most famous haunted house in America is the Winchester Mystery House in San Jose, California. Construction began on the Winchester Mystery House in 1884 shortly after the death of William Wirt Winchester, of the Winchester Repeating Arms Company. His widow, Sarah Winchester, was told by a psychic that members of her family had been killed by the ghosts of soldiers killed by Winchester rifles during the Civil War. She came to believe that she needed to continue building on the house to keep the evil spirits at bay. Consequently, construction on the house continued for the remainder of Sarah's life, which was thirty-eight years after construction began. As there were a number of sightings on the premises over the years, design details were included to fool the ghosts, including doors that opened into brick walls, stairs that went to the ceiling, Odd-sized stairways, and secret passages.

As anyone who has seen Beetlejuice can attest, not every haunting involves evil spirits. A prime example of this is the Pittick Mansion in Portland, Oregon. The Pitticks haunt the house by making it smell like roses (Georgiana Pittick's favorite flower) and moving pictures of Henry Pittick as a child from room to room. This one truly may be for the faint of heart.

The Villisca Axe Murder House is the site of an unsolved and most gruesome crime that occurred in Villisca, Iowa, in

1912. One fateful night an axe murderer entered the home of Josiah Moore and butchered Moore, his wife, their four children, and two other children who were visiting the house. The murderer was never identified nor apprehended. Many folks have reported seeing an axe-wielding ghost at the house over the years. As the crime and subsequent paranormal activity was well documented, over the years many tourists and fans of the paranormal have visited the house. One of the house's more well-known visitors was a paranormal activity investigator who in 2014 inexplicably was moved to stab himself in the chest.

Myrtles Plantation in St. Francisville, Louisiana, is a perfect storm of ghost-inducing activity (what were these idiots thinking?). It is a plantation where slaves were killed on the premises, and it was built on an Indian burial ground. It's haunted by at least twelve spirits. Its most often-viewed ghost is a former slave girl named "Chloe," who was murdered after having her ear lopped off. Many visitors have reported seeing her standing in windows.

Virginia Ferry Plantation House in Virginia Beach, Virginia, is not just haunted; it's haunted by the zaniest collection of spirits ever. It haunted-houses eleven ghosts and infamous witch, Grace Sherwood. There are ghosts of shipwreck victims, an angry slave (be careful, he's vengeful), a sad lady, a lady who keeps falling down the stairs, a guy who likes to paint. And several others. Among its most famous visitors is none other than Satan himself, who left his cloven hoofmark behind on the night of Grace Sherwood's death. Rumor has it that he was reclaiming her. Many have reported seeing her there subsequently.

The Porter Huntintgon Phelps Museum in Hadley, Massachusetts, is another dwelling haunted by friendly former residents. People who have stayed there have reported experiencing Mrs. Porter "tucking them in" at night. There are also reports of door latches moving up and down, despite no one being near the door. One of the editors of this book lived there while she was in graduate school. She didn't see any ghosts, but did hear many weird sounds at night.

No list of American haunted locations would be complete without at least one entry from New Orleans, which gives Salem, Massachusetts, a run for its money for the title "America's Spookiest Town." New Orleans doesn't disappoint. It houses The Sultan's Palace in the heart of the French Quarter. Plantation owner Jean Baptiste Le Prete owned the house in the mid-1800s. Since he was away at his plantation most of the year, he rented his house for a time to a young Turk who claimed to need the house for his brother, the Sultan. Upon moving in, the Turk brought in a harem of women and young men, and his many wives. He put guards on the gates and heavy drapes over the windows, so that no one could see what was going on inside. Folks passing by reported smelling opium and hearing orgies nearly round the clock. There were rumors swirling that the Turk kidnapped the Sultan's harem and stolen his treasure. One night someone broke in and dismembered everyone in the house, except for the Turk who was beaten and buried alive. The ghost of the Turk haunts the Sultan's Palace to this day. He reportedly burns incense and gropes women.

Having a ghost around definitely ups the spooky factor of a house, but some places just never seem spooky. Case in point: Hawaii's Iolani Palace. Iolani Palace was home to Hawaii's royal family throughout most of the nineteenth century. It's haunted by Queen Lili'uokalani who was imprisoned there for eight months following the overthrowing of the Hawaiian Government. The queen mostly wanders the hallways playing Hawaiian music (probably Aloha Oe, as it's Hawaii's most famous song, and she wrote it!). If she's going to manage to scare anybody, she's going to have to kick things up a notch, or two. Seriously, even Casper the Friendly Ghost has more game than Queen Lili'uokalani.

Asylums

Any fan of horror will tell you that mental institutions are chock full of evil spirits. From former residents who are exacting revenge for the unspeakable cruelties that were inflicted on them to ghosts that just enjoy the response they get from patients who are predisposed to be afraid, they flock to asylums like zombies flock to shopping malls. Three of America's most infamous asylums are the Trans-Allegheny Lunatic Asylum, the Waverly Hills Sanatorium, and the Athen's Lunatic Asylum.

Formerly known as the Weston State Hospital, the Trans-Allegheny Lunatic Asylum, which is located in Weston, West Virgina, housed the mentally ill from the 1860s till the 1990s. It was designed to house 250 patients, but, at its peak housed 2,400. It is certainly one of the institutions that served as inspiration for Season Two of *American Horror Story* (*American Horror Story: Asylum*). A number of murders occurred at the Trans-Allegheny Lunatic Asylum, including killingss of patients at the hands of patients, and murders of workers at the hands of patients. Reports of sightings include former patients as well as the ghosts of Civil War soldiers. None of this, however, compares to the really scary stuff that goes on there today: they still show the *Rocky Horror Picture Show* on Friday and Saturday evenings.

Waverly Hills Sanatorium in Louisville, Kentucky, has been dubbed by some as "America's most haunted location." And why wouldn't it be one of the most haunted places; so many residents died there that they actually installed a body chute so they wouldn't always be carrying corpses down the stairs (it was also the case that seeing lots of dead patients tended to rattle the other patients). The dead were dropped down the chute and directly into train cars. The great number of deaths were the result of tuberculosis. Later, however, the sanatorium was a home for geriatrics. During that era, a number of experiments were performed, including many involving electroshock therapy. Though it's been closed for several decades, folks report seeing ghosts, and smelling cooked food in the cafeteria. Of particular interest to paranormal investigators is Room 502. People have reported hearing voices say things such as "Get out." On two separate occasions nurses committed suicide in Room 502, one by hanging, and one by throwing herself out the window. The fifth floor is where the mentally ill tuberculosis patients were housed.

The Athens Lunatic Asylum (at various times called the Athens Hospital for the Insane, the Southeastern Ohio Mental Health Center, the Athens Mental Health Center (twice!), the Athens Mental Health and Mental Retardation Center, and the Athens Mental Health and Developmental Center—Sheesh!!!) in Athens, Ohio, is another creepy abandoned insane asylum. Like the Trans-Allegheny Lunatic Asylum, it was designed to house a limited number of patients, but ended up at over triple capacity. There were all sorts of cruel treatments (such as teeth-pulling, lobotomies, electroshock therapy, psychotic drug therapy, and so forth), and the inevitable hauntings that result. ALA's most famous ghost is a patient who locked herself in a room (the door was locked from the inside!), removed all her clothing, folded it up neatly, and then lay on the floor where she eventually died. She was found over a month later. A stain on the floor in the shape of this woman remains to this day.

Cemeteries

It goes without saying that cemeteries get haunted. It's unlikely that there exists a cemetery in the United States that hasn't had at least one paranormal activity reporting. I would go so far to say that any cemetery that isn't haunted just isn't doing its job.

Even with all this ghostly activity going on, three cemeteries rise above the rest: Hell's Gate/Oakwood Cemetery, Howard Street Cemetery, and St. Louis Cemetery #1.

This is another one that can get filed under "What were these guys thinking?" or better yet, "These guys were really asking for it!" The first mistake the folks from Hell's Gate/Oakwood Cemetery in Spartanburg, South Carolina, made was putting their cemetery on top of the town potter's field, where decades of indigent were buried. They followed that act by digging up the inhabitants of another local cemetery and putting them in Hell's Gate. Of course, there's the whole naming your cemetery "Hell's Gate" thing. Actually, quite a few cemeteries go by that moniker (Go figure!).

At any rate, it turns out that the dead like neither being dug up, nor having other dead folks placed on top of them. The proprietors aren't the only problem. For years a group of townsfolks have been holding satanic rituals (including breaking into graves!) at Hell's Gate. Paranormal investigators report all the "usual" stuff at Hell's Gate: orbs, voices, folks feeling like someone is touching them, and so on, but there are also reports of a more unusual phenomenon: batteries dying. The power seems to just drain out of cell phones and cameras. The most oft-seen ghost is a little boy holding a baseball.

Perhaps America's most beloved cemetery is Howard Street Cemetery in Salem, Massachusetts. It's right next to the Salem Jailhouse and it contains the graves of many involved in the Salem witch trials of the 1600s. It is rumored to be haunted by Giles Corey, whose story was immortalized in plays by Arthur Miller and Henry Wadsworth Longfellow. Corey was a farmer in Salem who took great interest in the Salem Witch Trials. He attended the trials regularly, along with his wife, Martha. Eventually Martha lost interest in the trials, and for some reason, Corey, accused her of witchcraft, and actually testified against her at her trial. Soon after, Corey was accused of witchcraft himself.

Corey refused to participate in his own trial, so he was taken to the cemetery, stripped naked, placed on the ground, and tortured by having a board with heavy stones placed on him. After four days of this he died. As he died he is reported to have shouted "Damn you Sheriff, I curse you and Salem!" Corey was known to have been a difficult man in life. In death, he was considerably worse. A number of mysterious deaths of Salem Sheriffs have been attributed to the ghost of Corey. One local claims to have seen a figure that looked just like him at the place where the Great Salem Fire of 1914 was started. Salem Resident and beloved writer Nathanial Hawthorne reports seeing Corey at the location of his death.

Perhaps America's most haunted cemetery is St. Louis Cemetery #1, in New Orleans. It's about the size of one city block, but over 100,000 bodies have been buried there (it only holds seven hundred tombs!). As far as really pissing off the dead goes, this, of course, is right up there with moving the dead and putting new dead folks on top of old dead folks. Mark Twain referred to it as "The cities of the dead." Fans of *American Horror Story* will be excited to learn that Marie Laveau, the Voodoo Queen (from *American Horror Story: Coven*), is buried there, and is reported to appear around the cemetery and near her former home. Some have claimed to have been shoved by her. As *American Horror Story* fans can attest, she was kind of nasty. Another ghost reported to haunt St. Louis Cemetery #1 is that of the sad Henry Vignes. Vignes's tomb was sold before he died, and he now has no home. Folks report a ghost that comes up to them and asks them whether they know where his tomb is. Similarly, there is a ghost there named Alphonse, who appears at funerals, asking folks to take him home. No one knows where this home is.

Prisons and Courthouses

Given the powerful combination of the sort of rotten souls that are prone to end up in prison, the cruel nature of some forms of punishment, the horrible living conditions in many prisons, and the mean-spirited nature of some of the prison guards and wardens, it is no surprise that many American prisons are haunted! Four of the worst (at least in terms of ghostly activity) are: Eastern State Penitentiary, Moundsville Penitentiary, Old Idaho Penitentiary, and the Old Montana Territorial Prison.

Eastern State Penitentiary in Philadelphia, Pennsylvania, was built in accordance with the Quaker beliefs that prisoners should be isolated and not have exposure to light except for the "light of God," which came via small skylights. Hence most prisoners were kept in dark solitary confinement, and when allowed to leave their cells, they were hooded. Later, really painful torture, such as chaining prisoners' tongues to their wrists, was commonplace. While eerie sounds, such as laughs and screams can routinely be heard through the now-closed prison, the most noteworthy event occurred when a locksmith opened a 140-year-old lock, to find himself paralyzed by a mysterious force while the faces of dozens of past prisoners appeared on the walls in front of him.

Moundsville Penitentiary in Moundsville, West Virginia, is haunted by a ghost known as the Shadow Man. The Shadow Man, a maintenance worker who was killed by inmates for reporting them to the guards, hides in the shadows and jumps out at people (hence the name). There are also reports of the circular entrance gate operating by itself, and bringing in new inmates. If you think about it, that must really suck. You are dead, you are a ghost, and now you are entering a prison. If it were me, I'd prefer to haunt that nice Hawaiian palace where the former queen plays her ukulele!

The Old Idaho Penitentiary in Boise, Idaho, does hauntings Idaho style. By that I mean that Idaho isn't exactly known for its pizzazz (hell, it's famous for potatoes!). At the Old Idaho Penitentiary, we find a red light that appears from time to time, visitors report developing sudden and mysterious headaches, and there are many reports of a ghostly former prisoner who tends to the rose garden. So why put this one on the list? It's the sheer volume of sightings. The place is lousy with paranormal activity.

By contrast, the Old Montana Territorial Prison in Deer Lodge, Montana, is truly terrifying! The number of prisoners who were executed there is actually exceeded by the number of prisoners who died in solitary confinement (there they call it "the hole"). Visitors to the now-closed prisoner routinely claim to hear voices calling to them from the solitary confinement cells. Spirits appear from every shadow, and there are reports of icy cold air manifesting itself.

Other Haunted Hotspots

Ghosts don't just confine themselves to the places they lived or were buried. There is no shortage of haunted hotels, ships, and assorted other public places. Here are some of the most notorious ghostly hot spots.

My personal favorite haunted hot spot on this list is the luxury ocean liner the *RMS Queen Mary*. The *Queen Mary* sounds English, so why is it on a list of American hauntings? It's because since 1967 it has been permanently docked in Long Beach, California. Why is it my favorite? Because I've visited it many times, taken all of the haunted ship tours, and on one recent occasion stayed there (it's a hotel now). Visitors on the *Queen Mary* frequently report seeing the ghosts of a maintenance worker, women near the pool area (where wet footprints often appear), a little girl with a teddy bear, a little girl who drowned, and an elegant woman in a white formal gown. One room, in particular, Room 340, is considered to be the most haunted room on the ship. In Room 340 a staff member was murdered some years back, and now the staff member haunts the room, turning on the faucets, pulling sheets off sleeping guests (this is not the standard use of sheets for ghosts), and banging on the walls. These things happened so frequently, that eventually they were forced to close the room for good.

Certainly, the most famous haunted hotel in America is the Stanley Hotel in Estes Park, Colorado. While it is not exactly famous for anything other than serving as the inspiration for Stephen King's novel *The Shining*, that doesn't mean that it's not a real hot spot of paranormal activity! In fact, King reportedly produced an outline of the book after spending just one creepy night in the Stanley. The most haunted room is Room 217 (the room that King stayed in). The legend is that it's haunted by a chamber maid, Mrs. Wilson, who was electrocuted during a lightning storm (other versions of the story have her being blown up while lighting a candle near a gas leak). She's often spotted cleaning up, folding bed sheets, and doing other chamber maid tasks. The second most haunted room is Room 428. Even though there is nothing above this room, except for the roof, guests report hearing furniture being moved around on the floor "above them." There's also a friendly cowboy known to haunt this room.

Much like on the *RMS Queen Mary*, there are also numerous reports of ghostly activity in the ballrooms and common areas, and reports of the ghosts of children appearing in the corridors.

Everyone in America is familiar with the Lizzie Borden story (it really helps to have your gruesome crime immortalized in a catchy nursery rhyme, if notoriety is your goal). In 1892 Lizzie Borden was accused of murdering both her parents with an axe. The house where the gruesome murders occurred is now the Lizzie Borden Bed and Breakfast in Fall River, Massachusetts (because, why not?). Guests claim to hear Lizzie's mother weeping at night, and see shoes moving by themselves.

Last, and actually least on our list, is Westminster College in Salt Lake City, Utah. Converse Hall is reportedly haunted by the ghost of a bride who died on her wedding day, not terribly far from Westminster. This haunting merits comment only because one of the editors of this book occasionally teaches in Converse Hall. She's not yet spotted the bride, but if she does, an updated second edition of this book will soon be in the works!

Bibliography

Alvarado, Denise . 2011. *The Voodoo Hoodoo Spellbook*. Weiser.

Anas, Brittany. 2016. The 7 Most Haunted Spots in the Stanley Hotel. *Tripsavvy* <www.tripsavvy.com/the-haunted-stanley-hotel-4108817>.

Aristotle. 1987. *De Anima (On the Soul)*. Penguin.

———. 1997. *Poetics*. Penguin.

———. 1999. *Nicomachean Ethics*. Hackett.

Augustine. 2008. *Confessions*. Penguin.

Auvil, Jennifer Plum. Top 10 Most Haunted Places. *Travel Channel* <www.travelchannel.com/interests/haunted/articles/top-10-most-haunted-places>.

Becker, Ernest. 2011. *The Denial of Death*. Souvenir Press.

Brooks, Rebecca Beatrice. 2011. The Curse of Giles Corey. *History of Massachusetts Blog* <http://historyofmassachusetts.org/the-curse-of-giles-corey>.

Cakebread, Caroline. 2016. Macbeth and Feminism. Shakespeare Institute, University of Birmingham.

Camus, Albert. 1991 [1942}. *The Myth of Sisyphus and Other Essays*. Vintage.

Cave, Stephen. 2012. *Immortality: The Quest to Live Forever and How It Drives Civilization*. Crown.

Colonial Ghosts. Ferry Plantation House. *Colonial Ghosts* <https://colonialghosts.com/ferry-plantation-house>.

Creepy Ghost Stories. Is the Queen Mary Ship Haunted? *Creepy Ghost Stories* <www.creepyghoststories.com/list/is-the-queen-mary-ship-haunted>.

Cupp, Kyle. 2014. A Postmodernist Defends Natural Law. *Ordinary Times: On Culture and Politics*.

Deren, Maya. 1953. *Divine Horsemen: The Living Gods of Haiti*. Thames and Hudson.

Diamond, Stephen A. 2009. Why Myths Still Matter (Part Four): Facing Your Inner Minotaur and Following Your Ariadnean Thread. *Psychology Today*.

Eckholm, Erik. 1986. What Is the Meaning of Cannibalism? *New York Times* <www.nytimes.com/1986/12/09/science/what-is-the-meaning-of-cannibalism.html?pagewanted=all>.

Ferri, Jessica. 2016. 50 Most Haunted Places in All 50 States. *HuffPost* <www.huffingtonpost.com/entry/50-most-haunted-places-in-all-50-states_us_57fbbcb4e4b0b665ad8186b3>.

Fandrich, Ina J. 2005. *The Mysterious Voodoo Queen, Marie Laveaux: A Study of Powerful Female Leadership in Nineteenth-Century New Orleans*. Routledge.

Ghosts and Gravestones. Most Haunted Places in America. *Ghosts and Gravestones Frightseeing Tour* <www.ghostsandgravestones.com/most-haunted-places-in-america.php>.

Goffman, Erving. 1963. *Stigma: Notes on the Management of Spoiled Identity*. Simon and Schuster.

Goldstein, Sasha. 2014. Paranormal Investigator Stabs Self During Visit to Iowa "Ax Murder" House Where 8 Killed: Cops. *New York Daily News* <www.nydailynews.com/news/national/man-stabs-visit-iowa-ax-murder-house-article-1.2002846>.

Goyette, John, Mark Latkovic, and Richard S. Myers, eds. 2004. *St. Thomas Aquinas and the Natural Law Tradition: Contemporary Perspectives*. Catholic University of America Press.

Haunted Rooms. 2017. Lizzie Borden's House Ghosts, Fall River, MA. *Haunted Rooms* <www.hauntedrooms.com/lizzie-bordens-house-ghosts-fall-river-ma>.

Kafer, Alison. 2013. *Feminist, Queer, Crip*. Indiana University Press.

Klemke, E.D., and Steven Cahn, eds. 2008. *The Meaning of Life*. Oxford University Press.

Kudler, Adrian Glick. 2015. The Real Story Behind LA's Most Famous and Mysterious Murder House. *Los Angeles Curbed* <https://la.curbed.com/2015/9/21/9920706/los-feliz-murder-house>.

Miller, Lee. 2002. *Roanoke: Solving the Mystery of the Lost Colony*. Penguin.

Montaigne, Michel Eyquem de. 1991. *The Complete Essays*. Allen Lane.

Montaldo, Charles. 2017. Haunting Ghost Stories of Eastern State Penitentiary. *ThoughtCo*. <www.thoughtco.com/haunting-ghost-stories-eastern-state-penitentiary-972975>.

Morton, Caitlin. 2016. The 20 Most Haunted Places in America. *Conde Nast Traveler* <www.cntraveler.com/gallery/the-most-haunted-places-in-america/1>.

Nola.com. Harem of Horror: Murder at the "Sultan's Palace." *Times-Picayune* <www.nola.com/haunted/index.ssf/2000/09/harem_of_horror_murder_at_the.html>.

Plato. 2000. *Timaeus*. Hackett.

Prinz, Roman. 2011. *Terror Management Theory: What Role Do Cultural World Views Play in the Cause and Prevention of Terrorism?* GRIN Verlag.

Rahula, Walpola. 1974. *What the Buddha Taught*. Revised and Expanded Edition. Grove.

Rampton, Martha. 2015. Four Waves of Feminism. Pacific University Oregon.

Roadtrippers. 2016. The Real Story of the Terrifying Stanley Hotel that Inspired "The Shining" (Ghost Update!). *Mapquest Travel* <https://travel.mapquest.com/2016/04/17/the-real-story-of-the-terrifying-stanley-hotel-that-inspired-a>.

Shakespeare, William. 2016 [1606–1607]. *Macbeth*. Penguin.

Smith, Angela M. 2012. *Hideous Progeny: Disability, Eugenics and Classic Horror Cinema*. Columbia University Press.

Solomon, Sheldon, and Jonah Lehrer. 2016. Fear, Death and Politics: What Your Mortality Has to Do with the Upcoming Election. *Scientific American* <www.scientificamerican.com/article/fear-death-and-politics>.

South Carolina Supernatural Investigations. Hell's Gate Investigation, Spartanburg SC. *SCSI* <https://scsupernatural.com/2014/02/13/hells-gate-investigation-spartanburg-sc>.

Taylor, Richard. 1999 [1967]. *Good and Evil*. Prometheus.

———. 2008. The Meaning of Life. In Klemke and Cahn 2008.

Taylor, Troy. Waverly Hills Sanatorium. *America's Most Haunted Places* <www.prairieghosts.com/waverly_tb.html>.

Theodore, Dorothy Deena. 2015. *Textbook of Mental Health Nursing*. Reed Elsevier.

True Hauntings of America. The Haunting of the Porter-Phelps-Huntington Mansion. *True Hauntings of America* <http://hauntsofamerica.blogspot.com/2007/10/haunting-of-porter-phelps-huntington.html>.

Wick, Jessica. 2016. A Tour of This Haunted Prison in Montana Is Not for the Faint of Heart. *Only in Your State* <www.onlyinyourstate.com/montana/haunted-prison-museum-mt>.

The Coven

Emiliano Aguilar is a vampire and a graduate of the Universidad de Buenos Aires (UBA), Facultad de Filosofía y Letras (Argentina), who feeds on popular culture, academic jargon, and scholarships. He has published chapters in *Orphan Black and Philosophy*, edited by Richard Greene and Rachel Robison-Greene; *The Man in the High Castle and Philosophy*, edited by Bruce Krajewski and Joshua Heter; and *Giant Creatures in Our World*, edited by Camille Mustachio and Jason Barr.

Fernando Gabriel Pagnoni Berns is a creature of the night who spends his waking hours writing blasphemous things for books such as *Horrors of War: The Undead on the Battlefield*, edited by Cynthia Miller, *To See the Saw Movies: Essays on Torture Porn and Post-9/11 Horror*, edited by John Wallis, or *Peanuts and Philosophy: You're a Wise Man, Charlie Brown!*, edited by Richard Greene and Rachel Robison-Greene, while drinking a blasphemous ambrosia (people call it vodka). He is currently writing a book about the Spanish TV horror series, *Historias para no Dormir*.

Matthew William Brake has an academic career defined by fear. He is a dual master's student in Interdisciplinary Studies and Philosophy at George Mason University—because he's afraid of getting his PhD. He also has a Master of Divinity from Regent University—but he's afraid of having a degree from Pat Robertson's university on his résumé. He has published numerous articles in the series *Kierkegaard Research: Sources, Recep-*

tion, Resources—and he's afraid they suck. He is a contributor for the Noetic podcast (www.noetic-series.com)—and he's afraid his voice sounds too nasal. He has chapters in *Deadpool and Philosophy* and *Mr. Robot and Philosophy*—and he's afraid that they're too contrived. Check out his blog at www.popularcultureandtheology.com—which he's afraid nobody ever checks out.

JACOB BROWNE can usually be found haunting the streets of Liverpool, England, muttering to himself about terrible visions and their dread implications. When the spirits leave him alone, he likes to read about phenomenology, madness, film studies, and anthropology. For the rest of the time, he does what he can to keep a healthy distance between himself and his old friends at Briarcliff.

GERALD BROWNING is an adjunct English instructor at Muskegon Community College and Grace Bible College. When he isn't teaching Composition, Literature, or Creative Writing classes, he is working on his own fiction or training in martial arts. His first novel, *Demon in My Head*, can be found on Amazon. He predominantly writes horror and mystery fiction, and cross trains in Ninjutsu, Judo, Tai Chi, and other martial arts. He has a beautiful wife and two amazing sons and a master's in English Studies, and he hopes to earn a black belt. When he isn't being creepy . . . well, we don't know because he's always quite creepy.

CARI CALLIS is an associate professor in Cinema and Television Arts at Columbia College Chicago, and currently working on a novel about Marie Leveaux. She's never met any of the Voodoo spirits personally, but only because she hasn't called upon them; she has no doubt they will answer when she does.

ROD CARVETH is an Associate Professor in Multimedia Journalism and Director of Graduate Studies for the School of Global Journalism and Communication at Morgan State University. He is a former cast-mate of Elsa Mars, having appeared in a snuff film with her. He still has his legs, though no one is able to vouch for his mind.

CHARLENE ELSBY is an Assistant Professor and Philosophy Program Director at Indiana University-Purdue University, Fort Wayne—at least, that is, until her Supremacy is recognized.

Richard Greene is a Professor of Philosophy at Weber State University. He also serves as Executive Chair of the Intercollegiate Ethics Bowl. He's co-edited a number of books on pop culture and philosophy including *The Princess Bride and Philosophy*, *Dexter and Philosophy*, *Quentin Tarantino and Philosophy*, *Boardwalk Empire and Philosophy*, and *The Sopranos and Philosophy*. Richard is sad that Mr. March never invites him to dinner.

Cherise Huntingford was inducted early on into the horror genre through her parents' questionable Bohemian ideas on censorship, and has been getting her pathological kicks from creative death scenes and jump-scares ever since. A Bachelor of Arts degree in psychology only convinced her that trying to deconstruct her twisted penchants is not much fun, so she turned English teacher instead and converted some impressionable teens into pretentious Poe fans. She has also written copious reviews for a London film magazine, along with a journal essay extolling the virtues of Leatherface and his power tool as the poster boy for psychic catharsis (in keeping with the rigors of exhaustive academic style, there may or may not have been a reference to nipple belts). *American Horror Story* has recently provided more attractive miscreants to write about, but luckily, subtlety is not its strong point, and Cherise has had hours of pleasure to elucidate the rich symbolism behind cherry-popping blood baths and people eating. Some folks just can't be helped.

Christopher Ketcham, PhD. With the help from Mara. Pieced together from the shredder. doctorat. resrch. ethic. busnes. Oh, the hell with it. Chris suffered but got the doctorate at UT Austin. Sure, he writes about the Buddha, but also Emmanuel Levinas who hates useless suffering. Who doesn't? Then again, Chris causes endless suffering of students at the University of Houston Downtown. How? You know, ethical dilemmas and the heartbreak of risk management. Well, that's about it. Did he get his 1,000th finger? Working on it . . .

S. Evan Kreider is an associate professor of philosophy at the University of Wisconsin, Fox Valley, and holds a PhD from the University of Kansas. His research interests include aesthetics and ethics, including their applications to pop culture. He also needs recommendations for a place to stay the next time he visits Los Angeles, and wonders if anyone has heard anything about this one art-deco hotel . . .

ROB LUZECKY is a lecturer at Indiana University-Purdue University, Fort Wayne. He has co-written numerous chapters for various Popular Culture and Philosophy volumes. His primary interests are in metaphysics and aesthetics, though lately he has taken a keen interest the ontologies of witches and creepy clowns. When he is not whistling a happy little tune as he strolls the halls of the local asylum, he finds himself in front of a room of strangers, where he speaks humorously about the stuff of horror stories.

CHRISTOPHE POROT is a graduate student, and Dean's Fellow recipient, at Harvard University. He is the managing editor, along with Dr. Charles Taliaferro, for a series on Philosophy of Religion in *Religious Studies Review*. He has also edited for *The Cambridge Companion to Platonism* and *The Stanford Encyclopedia of Philosophy*, and has multiple publications including those in *The European Journal for Philosophy of Religion*, *The Journal of Death and Anti-Death*, and volumes in the Popular Culture and Philosophy series. He's hoping to get away from the ghosts and ghouls that have been haunting his library and his laptop and eating all the food in his fridge.

ELIZABETH RARD is currently working on her PhD in Philosophy at UC Davis, and is a Philosophy Instructor at Reedley College. She must telecommute to meet these obligations, as she checked into the Hotel Cortez in 1947 and has been trapped there ever since. She had only intended to stay for a short while but unfortunately slipped in the shower and managed to snap her neck, leaving a horrible mess for the cleaning lady (although Miss Evers didn't seem to mind). Her hobbies include writing messages on foggy mirrors, leaving random slippery puddles of bath water on the lobby floor, and posting pictures of herself on the Internet wearing a variety of stylish shower caps.

RACHEL ROBISON-GREENE received her PhD in Philosophy at UMass Amherst. She is co-editor of *The Golden Compass and Philosophy*, *Dexter and Philosophy*, *Boardwalk Empire and Phi-*

losophy, *Girls and Philosophy*, *Orange is the New Black and Philosophy*, and *The Princess Bride and Philosophy*. She has contributed chapters to *Quentin Tarantino and Philosophy*, *The Legend of Zelda and Philosophy*, *Zombies, Vampires, and Philosophy*, and *The Walking Dead and Philosophy*. Rachel wonders what it would be like to be married to Twisty, but only when she isn't thinking of her husband.

SETH M. WALKER is a doctoral student at the University of Denver, studying religion, media, and popular culture. He regularly writes on topics in these areas—including volumes in the Popular Culture and Philosophy genre on *Jurassic Park*, *Orange Is the New Black*, *The Walking Dead*, and most recently *The Americans*. He edits an online magazine that engages the intersection between religion and popular culture: *Nomos Journal*. Unlike Fiona, he's not at all attached to his youth . . . just don't ask him why gray hairs disappear no sooner than they emerge.

Index